THE

VULNERABLE

INNOCENCE

By

Mark Anthony Buccat, RSW. Ph.D

COPYRIGHT @ 2023 THE VULNERABLE INNOCENCE
By Mark Anthony Buccat

All rights reserved. No part of this publication may be produced, distributed, or transmitted in any form or any means, including photocopying, recording, or other electronic or mechanical methods without the prior permission of the publisher and author, except in the case of brief quotations embodied in critical reviews and certain other commercial uses permitted by copyright law may be reproduced or used in any manner without the prior written permission of the copyright owner and publisher.

ISBN:
Hardbound-978-621-470-517-7
MOBI/KINDLE-978-621-470-518-4
Softbound/Paperback-978-621-470-519-1

Published by:
Poetry Planet Book Publishing House
Rosario, Pozorrubio, Pangasinan, Philippines
Contact Number: 09554960094
Email: maritesritumalta@gmail.com

TABLE OF CONTENTS

INTRODUCTION

I am aware of several researches done earlier on child prostitution highlighting the vulnerability of male children to sexual exploitation which is an issue related to the rights and protection of street children. However, focused attention and action to address the commercial sexual exploitation of boys is still lacking despite numerous local and foreign studies undertaken worldwide that referred to the exploitation of boys.

I have been a practicing Social Worker for almost twelve years since 2008. I am exposed to a lot of dilemmas encountered by street children, one of which is child prostitution, a phenomenon that traumatizes boys at a very young age. I experience difficulty in handling this kind of phenomenon especially at the start since my skills and understanding of this issue was limited. Motivating boys to change and improve themselves was not easy.

Working with different child welfare agencies that cater to children in need enhanced my skills and led me to a better understanding of the realities experienced by this sector.

My first working experience was with GMA Kapuso Foundation where I served as auxiliary social worker. This work developed my skills in basic case management especially in the area of protecting children from abuse. I followed this path and pursued helping abused and neglected children.

After a year, I moved to Unang Hakbang Foundation where I was assigned as Program Assistant. My work was focused on out-of-school youth and CICL (Children in Conflict with the Law). I explored the dilemmas encountered by these children such as those abandoned by both their parents and by their communities.

Another organization I worked for was Children's Chance for Tomorrow Foundation (CCTF) in Coron, Palawan. I was its Social Worker Trauma Therapist Facilitator. In this work, I learned different approaches in healing abused traumatic experiences thru art, music and play. These skills allowed me to assess and understand a child's traumatic experiences more easily, thus, enabling me to create proper intervention plans.

I am also the former Program Coordinator of Coomunity Based Program - Tondo at Onesimo Bulilit Foundation, Inc. catering to neglected and abused street children. This work provides me the opportunity to understand the phenomenon of street children and their dilemmas. I discovered that one of the major dilemmas concerning street children is neglect or abandonment by their parents and by their community which usually leads to unfortunate consequences such as prostitution.

These experiences made me pursue to publish this book. I hope to raise the awareness of the public on the plight of these unfortunate children who often end up victims of prostitution. I wrote this book because I am concerned. I feel that there is a need to reinforce the efforts of promoting and upholding the rights of boys to be protected against sexual exploitation. Being in this work for some time, I note that there has been a marked increase in the number of boys who are considered street dwellers engaged in prostitution.

Based on my encounter with young male prostitutes through my work, I have information that prostitution happens in different settings such as streets, malls or online. There's a thin line between exploring and getting coerced by another person who knows the trade. Here in the Philippines, young male prostitution is rapidly increasing because of different reasons that need further exploration. I have worked with male street children who are members of dysfunctional families and are engaged in prostitution in the community at Tondo, Manila.

Young male prostitution has a host of negative physical and psychological repercussions on the victim. These include reproductive health problems, anxiety, eating disorders, sexual dysfunction, substance abuse and school problems. Engaging in truancy and prostitution compounds them a long-term risk sexually-transmitted disease (Finkelhor, 2005).

Six male prostituted street children from Tondo, Manila, were willing enough to share their stories. Their age range is 13 – 17 years old. One of the six co-researchers is a high school graduate while the rest are elementary undergraduates. All are Catholics but none has a birth certificate for they are not registered in the National Statistic Office. Each journey is contained in their respective story which is presented on the first chapter of the book.

CHAPTER 1

THE VULNERABLE INNOCENCE JOURNEY

"Alpha"

"An innocent victim of abuse that leads him to a miserable life"

"Just call me Alpha. I am 17 years old, living in the street in Tondo Manila. My family came from Bulacan but I was born here in Manila. Currently, I am out-of school. I stopped schooling but recently I passed the Accreditation and Equivalency Exam with the help of a school and non-government organization. However, I did not pursue college. I want to be an Army if I have the chance to study at the Philippine Military Academy (PMA).

I am friendly and respectful of authority figures. I have a good relationship with my mother because she always guides me in every decision I made. My father died recently due to tuberculosis. I have two more siblings; I am the eldest. I also have good relationship with my brother and siblings. However,

most of the time, we are engaged in petty fights and arguments.

My mother provides us meals twice a day; sometimes they buy clothes for me as a present during Christmas.

I live in the street, thus, I always roam around in Plaza Morga. I meet a lot of friends including enemies belonging to other gangs. I have been living in the street for almost 13 years because our house was burned when I was four years old. I've been rescued by RAC (Reception Action Center) because I was sleeping in the street. I was admitted in Manila Boys Town Complex several times when I was younger.

I thought I was going to have a nice life believing the world was at peace. But, an unfortunate event took place that led me to become a victim of sexual abuse at age seven. Yes, I am abused and this is my story:

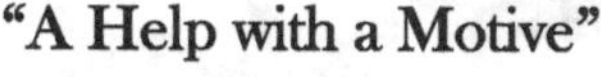

"A Help with a Motive"

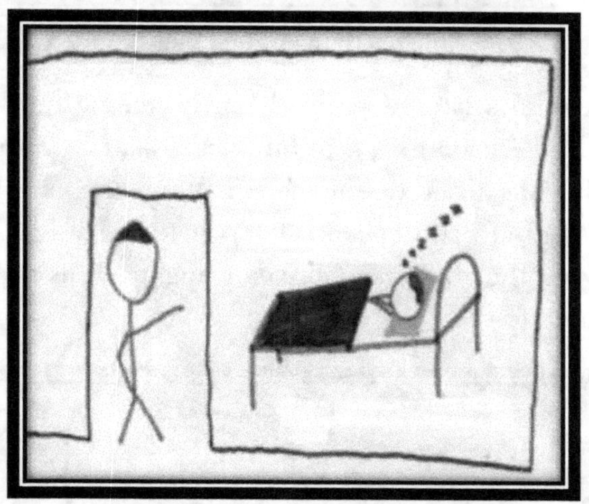

A help with a motive: Part 1

We stayed in one of my mother's friends named Christian when our house was burned. We had already been living in the street for a couple of years then. Quite old, Christian was very nice to me.

One time, Christian and I were left alone in his house. While I was fast asleep, I noticed him masturbating in front of me. Since I had no idea what he was doing at that time, I ignored him.

A help with a motive: Part 2

Few days later, I noticed him watching me while I was taking a bath. I tried to splash him with water to go away but he remained. I was afraid he might enter the bathroom. It would be difficult for me to run because I was naked. I was also afraid to tell to my mother because Christian might tell us to leave. We had nowhere to go.

A help with a motive: Part 3

What he did became a reason for me to start avoiding him. After 2 days, he tried to apologize for what had happened. He invited me to the store to buy drinks and snacks. Despite the kindness shown, I felt so uncomfortable and afraid because I didn't know what his motive was.

A help with motive: Part 4

After buying snacks, we went back to his house. My parents were busy looking for a job during that time and I didn't have any siblings yet.

He invited me to watch pornographic video with a male and female having sex. While watching this kind of movie, I was so afraid especially when he started to take off his clothes and became totally naked. He masturbated beside me and started to take off my clothes. He said he will just do the things we were watching and started to lick my private part. I felt ashamed and afraid with what happened. I had no guts to tell my mother so I ran away and never returned. When my mother asked me the reason for not going back to the house of his friend, I just responded that I was happier living in the street with my friends even if in reality I was not.

Yes, I am a victim of sexual abuse at a very young age and I am just one of the million children who became victims of this realistic issue in this world. I remained silent about the incident because I knew it will destroy my life and even my manhood. I blamed myself for what had happened and asked God if I should live. I further asked why God must make an unsafe and dangerous world for children like me.

I started to hate myself while fighting the nightmare that turned out to be a reality. I learned using my private body by selling it at a low price just to earn money to sustain my vices such as marijuana, cocaine, solvent, cigarette and alcohol. These vices were the only means to forget hating myself with what happened. I was aware it had consequences. In fact, I was destroying my life by engaging in prostitution. I was taking risk with every customer I encountered because I allowed myself to do everything they wanted such as oral and anal sex. Still, I needed to do those things to sustain my vices. I knew I destroyed my life.

"One Day Changed It All!"

One day changed it all: Part 1

I was twelve when it happened to me the first time. It was raining that day and I was just standing beside Plaza Morga. I was watching my friends playing gate ball (a similar game of golf but done in the street/plaza) at around 8:00 in the evening. At that time, I was already using marijuana. I was also into other vices such as smoking and drinking alcohol at that time which was an influence from my peers who were likewise living in the street.

One day changed it all: Part 2

Someone called me and introduced himself as Dan. I knew him before because I saw him interacting with some of the kids in the street. I was aware that he was paying kids for sex. Dan influenced me to do this kind of work. He was a gay, quite old at age 50. Because of my sexual abuse experience, I thought that it can also help me sustain my vices. I was convinced that I was going to enter the world of prostitution.

Dan was my first-ever costumer. He promised to pay me PhP400 pesos in exchange of oral sex. I knew I needed money to buy drugs and support my vices. Though hesitant to take the offer, I could not refuse.

One day changed it all: Part 3

He asked me to go to a dark alley near DPS. Dan immediately took off my shorts and did oral sex. I felt ashamed and dirty; but, I experienced pleasure. It was my second time to experience having sex with a gay since I was seven when Christian abused me.

One day changed it all: Part 4

After a couple of minutes, he gave me the money. I immediately ran away from him. I used the money in the internet shop where I played all day. I am afraid to go back in the Plaza Morga because I feel ashamed and afraid if someone knew what happened. I returned in Plaza Morga after 4 days.

What happened made me pursue this kind of work. I met new friends who I knew were also into prostitution. I asked them information where to get costumers, how much was the usual rate and what were the techniques in making the costumers satisfied.

Yes, I learned a lot and continued this kind of dirty job. At the same time, I continued using drugs. My mother knew all the time I was begging in the streets all the time and I used to stay up late. She didn't know I was engaged in prostitution.

"A Package that Cannot Be Refused"

A package that cannot be refused: Part 1

While in Plaza Morga waiting for a customer, a 40-year old man named Philip, sat beside me. I knew him for almost a week because he gave me money and food including cocaine without any exchange in return. At that moment, I just took valium and I felt so high.

A package that cannot be refused: Part 2

Philip asked me if I wanted to have sex with him and offered a PSP (Playstation Portable), PhP1,260.00 pesos and 3 tea bags of marijuana. I was afraid and confused. I did not know what to do. "Nanghihinayang" with the offer, I decided to accept it and do the things he wanted me to do.

A package that cannot be refused: Part 3

A package that cannot be refused: Part 4

He invited me to go with him to the dark alley of DPS near the police precinct No. 2 behind the 2 big trucks because according to him instead of renting a room in a hotel he will just give me the money.

While we were in the dark alley, he took off my pants and put condom into my private part. He started doing oral sex. I experienced pleasure but I had regrets by not being able to explain. After that, he asked me to do anal sex with him. I started feeling numb because I was high with the valium I took earlier. After everything, he fulfilled his promise to give the items. I decided not to see him again. Sadly, I also sold the PSP to my friend to be able to purchase more marijuana.

A Friend or a Customer?

A friend or a customer? Part 1

At a young age of 14, I was an experienced child prostitute. Alone, I was on my way to Isetan-Recto at around 1:00 in the morning. I was afraid but excited everytime I did it because it was either I was making money or a police could catch me because it was curfew.

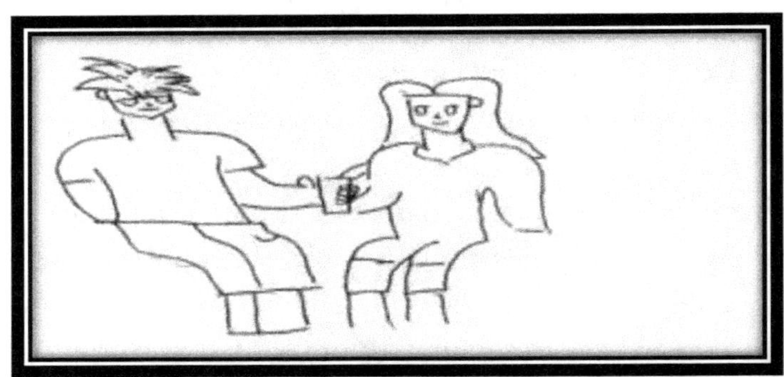

A friend or a customer? Part 2

Suddenly, I saw my gay friend, Eric, at Plaza Morga. Eric was only 12 years old. He knew I was a prostitute. He asked me what the feeling of having sexual intercourse is. He also asked me to do anal sex with him and was willing to pay me P100.00 pesos. I didn't refuse because he was my friend. I gave what he

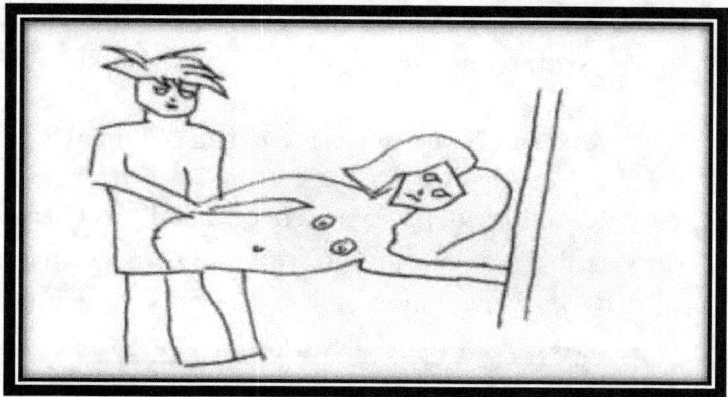

asked.   **A friend or a customer? Part 3**

We went to the dark alley beside Mary Johnston Hospital where we were covered by a big truck. I asked him to take off his pants and hold on the post. I slowly put my private part into his anus. It was a pity for he was hurt and he cried. Despite what happened, he refused to stop what I was doing.

A friend or a customer? Part 4

When I was done doing what he wanted, he gave me a P100.00 peso bill. However, he asked money from me so to buy coconut juice and mefenamic. According to him, in doing unsafe sex without condom there is a need to drink coconut juice. Since I knew him, I gave him P15.00 pesos. Therefore, the amount I received from him was only P85.00 pesos. I felt betrayed. I was disappointed with what happened.

"Anyone can be a customer, even an old man!"

Another unforgettable experience while I was engaged in prostitution was having sex with a 70-year old man. At that time, I was addicted to playing online games. My vices were lessened.

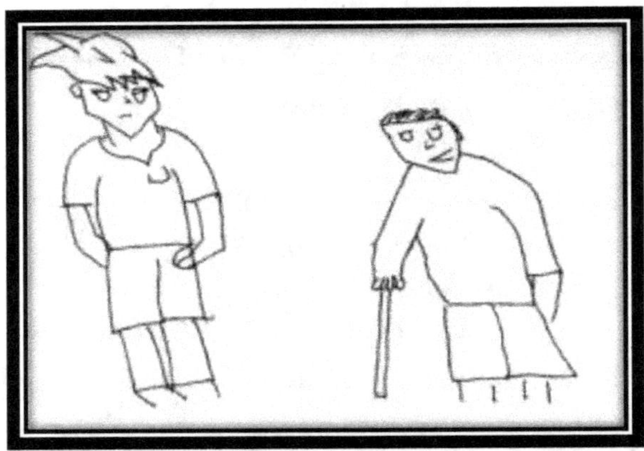

Anyone can be a customer even an old man! Part 1

At around 2:00 in the morning, an old man asked a direction going to Juan Luna. At this time, I was a bystander along Plaza Morga. I was waiting for a costumer who will pick me up. I worked alone; I had no pimps or someone with me. I told him the direction immediately. He asked me how much.

Honestly, I was disgusted when I heard him say it because he was too old and I could not imagine having sex with him. However, since I was addicted with online games, I accepted his offer.

Anyone can be a customer, even an old man! Part 2

He showed me a P500 peso bill and offered me P350.00 pesos just to do oral sex. I immediately accepted the offer and went to the dark alley of DPS where we usually bring our customers.

Anyone can be a customer, even old man! Part 3

I hastily took off my pants and he started doing oral sex with me. It seemed that the old man was hungry doing it. I experienced pleasure but with disgust.

Anyone can be a customer even an old man! Part 4

As soon as we were done, he gave me the P500.00 peso bill but asked that I give him a change of P150. I never came back. I went straight to the computer shop.

A regular customer I can count on: Part 1
"A Regular Customer I Can Count On"

Jessica, a 'shemale' aged 30, is a regular customer of my friends. S/He works in the market in Pavia selling vegetables and fruits. S/he has a breast because of injecting hormones by herself. Whenever I need money to buy alcohol, marijuana and solvent, I usually offer my body to him/her.

The last time I offered my body to him/her in exchange of money was when I was 16 years old.

A regular customer I can count on: Part 2

Jessica accepted my invite and offered only P250.00 pesos. S/He told me that we can have sex in his house so that we don't need to pay for an inn. I was drunk and high at that time so I did not hesitate to take the offer.

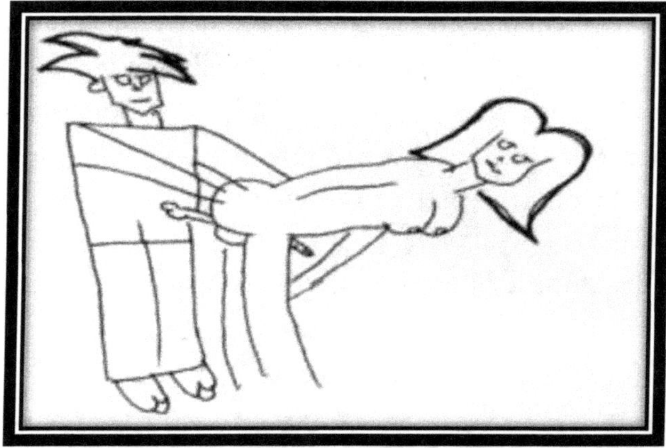

Figure 1. A regular customer I can count on: Part 3

We proceeded to his/her house in Pavia. Upon reaching the house, we took off our shirt. Jessica had breasts but s/he had penis. She looked like a "mananangal" (half human body, half monster). I did anal sex with him/her without using condom. It took me long to finish because I was high with drugs.

Figure 2. A regular customer I can count on: Part 4

After the sex encounter, I got the P250.00 pesos. I immediately purchased two tea bags of marijuana worth P100.00 pesos and 4 tablets of volume costingP23.00 pesos each. I could easily purchase this item at Bando 45 Store near Perpekto High School. I also purchased amoxicillin to make sure I will not acquire HIV or STD.

"An Encounter with a Fake Woman!"

Figure 3. An encounter with a fake woman: part 1

I met Jessie, a 30-year old 'shemale,' in Plaza Morga only last year. I was 16 then. Along the street, s/he called me and asked if I am engaged in prostitution. I immediately answered, yes. I noticed her big breasts and so I thought s/he was a real woman. S/he offered P500 which I did not refuse. S/He proudly told me that seldom I will encounter customers like him/her. That made me a little bit curious especially the way s/he looked.

Figure 4. An encounter with a fake woman: Part 2

We went to a hotel in Divisoria called, "SMILEY." It's a place where some of my prostituted friends do business. We took a room for 3 hours' worth P190.00 pesos. I was used to the place because I already checked-in the place several times before with previous costumers. They just gave the security guard some tips so he will allow us to go inside the hotel even if we were minors.

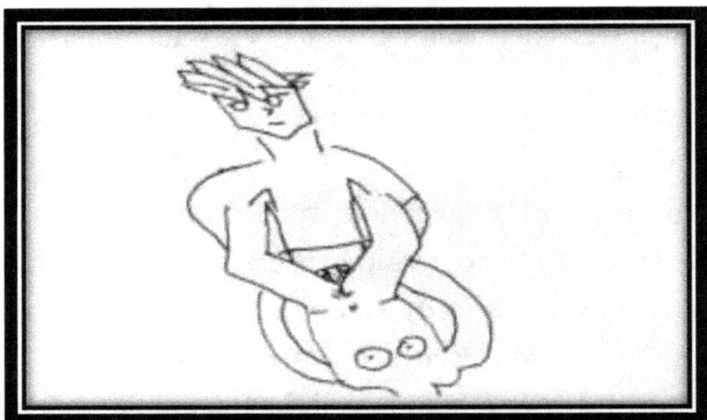

Figure 5. An encounter with a fake woman: Part 3

Jessie asked me to start taking off my shirt which I did. S/he also started doing oral sex. When s/he started removing his/her clothes, I was shocked! She had breasts and vagina which she said was done in Japan long time ago while s/he was working there. Shocked and amazed, I could not believe it was possible for a male to have vagina.

Figure 6. An encounter with a fake woman: Part 4

After the sexual encounter, s/he gave me theP500 pesos as agreed. I immediately purchased a Nokia 6300 phone which was my first-ever cell phone. I felt so happy and accomplished during that day. Sadly, though, my mother pawned it forP200.00 pesos and I never had the chance to redeem it.

Honestly, I know that what I was doing was not the right way to forget my traumatic experiences. However, I could not think of other things that I can do because I grew up in a world where hopeless people live. This has been how I perceived things since I was young.

I can get support from my friends who are doing similar kind of work. Gerald always protected me every time my mother gets mad at me. Jonjon is the person who I can lean on during fights with gangs. Elking provides me financial support whenever I need money. Nilo, who is my best friend, is always with me all the time especially when we play games online. Sometimes I also get into fights with Kervin who is also a friend.

I am hot-tempered. I get easily irritated even with small things. But I have adult friends who I associate with. Brother Jobert is a person I truly trust even with my dirty secrets. Brother Pedi provides me advice and sometimes teaches me different positions in terms of sex. Moreover, my girlfriend, Jesica, understands and accepts me as I am.

I admit my shame in the community where I grew up. When my parents knew what was happening to my life they had difficulty accepting me for engaging in such a dirty job. Later, however, they accepted me. I felt it as days went by. I sought their acceptance. Since that day, my life changed.

My friends used to tell me that things already happened and we cannot do something about it anymore. I just need to move on. I felt their encouragement and support.

I thought that the only way to help prostituted street children is to protect them from sexual abuse. It is one reason why there still rapid increase of prostituted children. They are abused!

To help me out of prostitution, I need some leisure and an income-generating project like the "piso-net" (computer shop). This will help me from thinking of means to get into any vice because I will become busy. At the same time, the work that I will engage in must provide me some pleasure.

I believe that my experiences in prostitution were risky. However, despite refusal to be into it, being a victim of sexual abuse brought me to this kind of situation and I could be in this situation until the end."

"Egou"
"A boy who survives to fulfil the needs of his family"

"I am Egou, 17 years old living in the street in Tondo Manila. I have no birth certificate and I only finished Grade 5 because I helped my mom to earn money in Plaza Morga by engaging in prostitution. My father abandoned us since the day when I was born. My mother started dating other guys in the street who became my step-father. I have two half-sisters.

My step-father died three years ago due to kidney failure. He was always drunk. He used to beat my mother. Most of the time, he also beat me.

I dreamt of pursuing my studies but my priority was to help my mother raise my two half-sisters. I was the only man left in the family. Hence, it was my responsibility to provide their needs. Sadly, one of my half-sisters died at a young age of nine in

2014 due to tuberculosis. I was ashamed of myself because I could not protect them. Moreover, I was not able to provide medicine for my half-sister. My mother is a laundry woman earning P300 per week. She was too weak and sickly but she did not want to disclose her illness to me because she did not want me to worry. Despite her situation, she still tried to provide me food and medicine when the need arises.

I have few friends in Plaza Morga namely: Jonathan, who protects me whenever I encounter riots and fights on the street; Vincent, who provides me medicine whenever I have STD (Sexually Transmitted Disease); and, Gina, who motivates me to stop engaging in prostitution. My other friends like Jasper, Mark, Miki and Marjun are bad influence. They were the ones who provoked me to get costumers. They taught me different ways of dealing with the costumers. Most of the time, I was with them.

I am Egou; I feel lost and hopeless because I need to help my Mother and half-sister to live but don't know where to get help. The only way to do this is to sell my body for sex. This is my story.

"The Beginning of a Miserable Life"

Figure 7. The beginning of a miserable life, part 1

I was 14 years old when I started to engage in prostitution. My half-sister needed medicine for tuberculosis; I didn't know how to help her. I was alone in the middle of the night. It was exactly 7:00 in the evening that time. Someone talked to me and introduced himself as Dan.

Figure 8. The beginning of a miserable life, part 2

I knew Dan for a long time because I always see him beside Sto. Nino Church selling oils and medicines. He was 36 years old and gay. He asked me if I wanted some money. I was surprised because it was like an answered prayer. He asked me to go with him so I can earn money. He treated me to dinner. I remember eating 'adobong baboy' and vegetables. After dinner in one of the restaurants beside the church, he asked me to go to a motel in Avenida. Called Luxury Motel at that time, I had really no idea that he was inviting me for sex. I was innocent at that time and thought that he would be asking a helping hand related to his work. I had no choice. I really wanted the money so bad for my half-sister's health condition. He offered me P500.00 pesos to satisfy him in bed.

Figure 9. The beginning of a miserable life: Part 3

When we arrived in the luxury motel in Avenida, he paid P180 pesos for 13 hours. I was shocked when he started taking off my clothes. He asked me to follow him and do what he asked me to do so I can have the P500.00 pesos. I really didn't like what we were doing. I kept thinking about the health condition of my half-sister and besides I can no longer back out from the deal. He started to do oral sex with me which took long.

Figure 10. The beginning of a miserable life: Part 4

After that we took some rest and slept. I felt numb afterwards and I could not explain my feelings. On one hand, I was happy because I was going to have money. On the other hand, I was sad. Shame poured my emotions. He gave me P500.00 pesos. Immediately, I bought medicines for my sister. But it was too late. When I went home, I saw my sister lying on the street lifeless.

After what happened, I felt dirty and ashamed of myself. I had no strength to say it to my mother or even to my other half-sister. So I tried to use weeds and sniffed glue to forget what happened to my life. I felt miserable. I was wrong. It worsened my situation and slowly destroyed my life. I became addicted to drugs and continued engaging in prostitution to support my vices. I didn't know what to do. Prostitution became my way of life. It was my means to live and fulfill my vices.

"I Lost My Virginity to an Old Seaman"

Figure 11. I lost my virginity to an old seaman: Part 1

One time, I went to Isetan Department Store with my friends. It was around 3:00 in the afternoon. We were playing video games at the 3rd floor of the mall. I was 16 years old then. Suddenly, a 40-year old man asked me if I can have sex with him. I agreed since I needed money that time. The guy was a retired seaman.

Figure 12. I lost my virginity to an old seaman: Part 2

The old seaman gave me P500 pesos as down payment and assured me to pay fully later. He told me that he will give additional P1,200 if I come with him. I was excited because I can use the money to help my mother to start a small business. He didn't told me his name so I had no idea who he was. We went to a hotel near Isetan. I forgot what it was called but I was sure it was just behind the mall.

Figure 13. I lost my virginity to an old seaman: Part 3

When we were in the hotel, he started taking his clothes off and mine, too. He asked me to take a bath with him. I agreed. We were rented in a room where we had sex for about two to three long hours. He told me to follow him and do all the favors he asked of me. He started licking my body and did oral sex. He asked me to do the same with him otherwise I will not get the money. So I had no choice but to do as he said. He asked me to insert my penis to his ass and after doing so he did the same to me. It hurt and so I cried. It made me feel so sad and I regretted doing it. We both had no condoms doing the sex. He told me that it would be his last time to stay in Manila because he was going abroad. He said I should feel luckier.

Figure 14. I lost my virginity to an old seaman: Part 4

After checking out of the room, he gave me the P1,200 pesos. Despite the pain I experienced, I still feel very happy because I was able to help my mother.

We parted ways. I went back to my friends in the mall but they were no longer there so I went home instead. I immediately gave the P1,000 pesos to my mother who was very happy when I handed it over to her. I used the remaining amount to purchase new clothes and drugs.

She did not even bother asking me where got it. She started a small grocery along the street with cigarettes and candies as among the goods for sale.

"A Birthday Costumer"

Figure 15. A birthday customer: Part 1

My last experience in prostitution was in June 2015. It was my birthday and we had no money to celebrate it so I tried to look for gays. It was around 10:00 in the evening when I saw an old man in Plaza Morga. He asked if I wanted to come with him to buy clothes. I didn't refuse his invitation since he was just asking for a companion.

Figure 16. A birthday customer: Part 3

After buying clothes and dining-in in Jollibee-Divisoria, he asked me if I wanted P600.00 pesos in exchange for sex. I immediately accepted his offer without hesitation. He asked me to come with him in the dark alley along Plaza Morga. It was around P12:00 midnight when we found a spot for sex.

Figure 17. A birthday customer: Part 3

In the dark alley, he started taking off my shorts and did oral sex. After several minutes, he asked me to do anal sex with him. He started putting saliva on my penis and inserted his ass. We didn't use condom. We had sex for almost 2 hours in this dark alley and I felt numb and dirty, full of saliva and disgusted with what I was doing.

Figure 18. A birthday customer: Part 4

After sex, he immediately gave me the P600 pesos and abandoned me in the dark alley. I was happy when I received the money. I used it to purchase chocolates which I gave to my sister. I also bought a small cake in the bakery to celebrate my birthday.

I had a good relationship with my mother despite knowing that I was engaged in prostitution. Still I am ashamed to face the community for what I am doing. If I could have other means to earn money, probably I would stop engaging in prostitution. I was only an elementary undergraduate and had limited opportunity to engage in stable job.

I know how difficult life is and there are a lot of risks to survive. I know how it feels to have sex to a stranger even if you don't like it. But I need to keep fighting to live and to fulfill my needs."

"Jaymar"
"Influenced by peers who took deadly risk to fit in"

"I am Jaymar, 14 years old. My miserable life is the result of influence by peers. We have a house but I always stay in the street because my parents used to hurt each other. My parents used to abuse me physically whenever they were drunk and high on drugs. I only have one sibling, a sister named Jelisa who is 10 years old. She is the favorite of my parents. Despite the abuse I experienced from my parents, I believe they were only protecting me and it was for my own good. However, I didn't listen.

I have been living with my friends in the street for almost 3 years. With them, I learned a lot of bad things including prostitution and different vices. I became more vulnerable from different illness such as cough, colds and even UTI (Urinary Tract Infections). I felt so unsafe living in Plaza Morga because I experienced being accused as a theft. Moreover, I was hit by a bottle of soft drinks in my head. Despite this danger, I feel safe and protected by my peers and I treated them as my real family.

I only finished grade 3 and stopped attending formal school last 2012. I ran away from home because my father hit me with a thick wood in the different parts of my body when he learned that I sniffed glue. From that day on, I didn't even bother going back home. So I stopped going to school. I wanted to be a pilot someday...but I guess it will remain a dream.

My life was totally changed when I lived on the street. I realized a lot of things and learned to be independent. Begging money and even foods in Tondo is fun because a lot of people admire my looks. They give me money immediately. Some people asked if I wanted to be an actor while others wanted to adopt me.

My friend, Kyle (13 years old), asked me why I don't use my face to earn from gays rather than beg on the street. He told me he did it twice so it's no big deal at all. He also said the gays only do oral sex for pleasure. At the same time, I earn money. At first, I was hesitant to follow what he was doing but I realized that it was the world I chose – to be independent and to survive living alone. I thought it will give me pleasure and money without any consequences. But I was totally wrong. Recently, I was diagnosed with STD (Sexually Transmitted Disease). Only then I realized how miserable the path I took in my journey.

"Partners in Crime"

Figure 19. Partners in Crime: Part 1

While walking in the street one day with Kyle, both of us 13 years old, at around 11:36 in the evening, we saw a gay. Kyle asked me to talk to the gay to ask money. At first, I was shy and afraid because he might hurt us. Suddenly, the gay called us so we approached him.

Figure 20. Partners in Crime: Part 2

He introduced himself as Lindon, 30 years old and living in Kagitingan Street. He asked us if we wanted money, to which we immediately replied, yes. He asked us to go to the dark alley behind parked trucks. Kyle was very happy because he knew we will have money. On my part, I was so afraid because it was my first time.

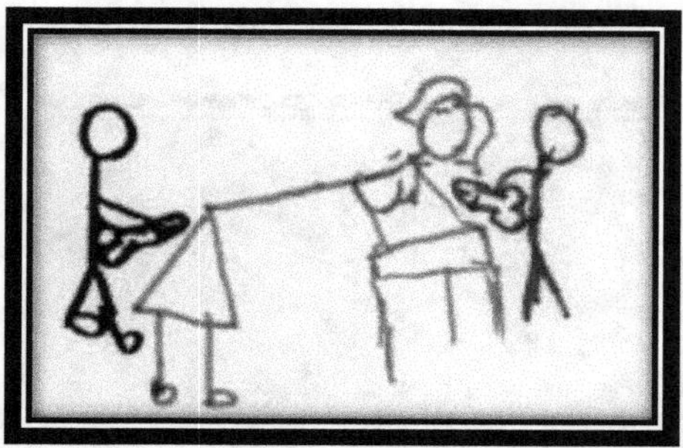

Figure 21. Partners in crime: Part 3

When we were in the dark alley, Lindon started to remove our shorts and licked our private parts. I was so disgusted especially when he asked me to put my penis into his anus. Having sex with him lasted for 30 minutes without using any condoms.

Figure 22. Partners in Crime: Part 4

After having sex with Lindon, we ate late dinner at "tapsilogan." It was past 12 midnight that time. He tried asking many things about us. After eating, he gave us P300 pesos. It felt great receiving my first earning from prostitution. We went immediately to the computer shop to play crossfire. We also bought solvent and cigarettes.

"Numbness, Guilt and Shame"

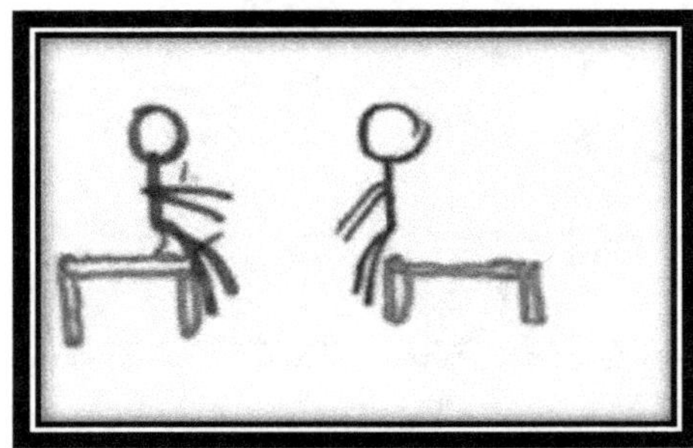

Figure 23. Numbness, guilt and shame: Part 1

It was exactly 11:56 in the evening in Plaza Morga when I and Reymond (15 years old) sniffed glue. I was 13 years old when we had a very funny conversation. We had jokes. Then we bought solvent worth P5 in Binondo.

Figure 24. Numbness, guilt and shame: Part 2

Figure 25. Numbness, guilt and shame: Part 3

Suddenly, a gay called Reymond asked us if we wanted money. This gay introduced himself as Jong-jong and an old customer of Reymond. He asked us to go with in his house in Don Bosco C.P. Garcia Street where we can have sex. At first, I was hesitant to come with him because he was a stranger and he might not allow us to leave the house. However, Reymond motivated me to come with them.

When we arrived in Jong-jong's house, he started kissing Reymond and slowly removed our clothes off. I really felt numb this time because we just had sniffed glue and was feeling very high. Jong-jong started to lick our penis. He tried to kiss me but I refused. We had sex for only 20 minutes.

Figure 26. Numbness, guilt and shame: Part 4

After having sex with Jong-jong, he gave us P500 pesos. At that very moment, I didn't feel happy and excited at all. All I felt was numbness, guilt and shame for what I've done. While we were heading for Plaza Morga, Reymond asked me to look for other gays to earn money but I refused. We separated ways. I bought slippers and clothes at the night market afterwards.

"A Risky Encounter"

Figure 27. A risky encounter: Part 1

Only two weeks ago, my friend, Long-long (16 years old), and I were roaming around the street at around 12:46 am when a cross dresser gay who introduced himself as Lina and around 35 years old, called us. I was already 14 years then. He asked us if we wanted money and we answered yes.

Figure 28. A risky encounter: Part 2

Suddenly, Lina changed his mind. He wanted to see first our penis if we were already circumcised. He was shocked when he saw our huge penis! He asked us to follow him under the bridge of Rawis where there were no people around, only stationary jeepneys in the terminal.

Figure 29. A risky encounter: Part 3

It was very dark. One can hardly recognize another. He sat in a small chair and asked us to remove our shorts. He licked our penis. It was a pleasure. He asked us to put both our both penis into his anus without using condoms. Having sex with Lina lasted for 40 minutes. I guess this was where I got infected with STD.

Figure 30. A risky encounter: Part 4

After having sex with him, he gave us P350.00 pesos each. He told us that was the only money he got. We separated ways. Reymond and I immediately went to a computer shop and play the whole morning. After playing, we ate breakfast and bought solvent in Binondo. We were so high the whole day and it felt great.

Actually, my parents and my sister had no idea that I was engaged in prostitution for a living. Whenever I go home, my parents sensed I was taking solvent because of the smell in my mouth. They tried asking me to stop but I refused. My parents tried to raise me well and be a good child. They taught me to help others, to respect other people, and to avoid peers who are bad influence. I refused following any of them.

When I reached a point where I acquired STD, my peers advised that I seek the help of a social worker. I approached Sir Mark for help. I asked for medicine for my illness. He assisted me to the hospital and immediately informed my parents about my condition. Currently I am thankful to God for the love and acceptance from my parents despite being a hard headed child.

I want to pursue my studies but my miserable experiences are trying to prevent me from doing it. I no longer want to engage in prostitution. This is a new beginning of my life and I am not going to waste it again."

"Kuya"
"A gambler gambles his life just to fulfill his vices"

"You can call me Kuya, 16 years old. I was born full of sorrow and pain. I tend to think God has given many bad omens to the world which I seem to assume we all have it. Despite these and the extreme hardships I encounter, however, I am happy because I am with my family and we can eat meals on time. That is something I thank God for.

I am the eighth child among thirteen (13) children. My father works in in "karerahan" as one of its personnel. He earns PhP300 a day while my Mother is a laundry woman earning

PhP500 a week. Even if both are working, their income is not sufficient to provide our basic needs. That's why we live on the streets near the Plaza Morga. I am even thinking that maybe will die on the streets just like the others. I have a good relationship with my mother because she is very understanding and she provides my needs. However, my father doesn't even care for us. He is always drunk and is addicted to vices. This has been the situation since I was a child. We eat two meals a day. My mother buys medicine when we get sick.

I've been living in the street for almost eight years. Since my siblings (brothers and sisters) have multiplied, my parents had difficulty sustaining the rent of our house; thus, forcing us to live in the street. Despite negligence by my father of his responsibilities as a father and the limited financial resource we have, my mother was able to enroll four of my siblings including me. After graduating in elementary, I decided to stop schooling because I didn't have a birth certificate which is one of the important document requirements to enroll in High School. Moreover, I was influenced by my peers not to pursue my studies and instead live with them totally in the street.

Nowadays, trustworthy people are few. The only people you can lean on are your parents. I experienced a lot of traitors among my friends while living in the street.

Kervin influenced me to engage in prostitution. A year older than I, he is also a prostituted child. According to him, the easiest way to earn money is the kind of job we do. He said that with it, I can buy the things I want and do the things that provide pleasure. He even told me that I have the looks that can hook-up a lot of gays including old ladies. Meanwhile, Joshua taught me how to sniff solvent and had me addicted to computer. Usually, I stay all night just playing games with them. We also gamble on the streets. Sometimes, the barangay policemem catch us doing this. I engaged in prostitution for the sake of doing things we wanted to do. This is the beginning of my experience.

"A Government Employee is my Customer"

Figure 31. A government employee is my customer: Part 1

I was only twelve years old and my friend, Joshua, ten years old, then. We were roaming around the Plaza Morga looking for ways to earn money so we can play computer games. It was 10:00 in the evening and I was still going to school at that time.

Figure 32. A government employee is my customer: Part 2

Roaming led us to Cristobal Street. One of the employees of Atienza (previous Mayor) named Michael, a 40-year old gay, approached him. He asked me how old I was and what I was looking for. I immediately responded that we needed money so we can play computer. Then suddenly he asked me silently if I wanted to have sex with him for P50.00 pesos. Since I needed money badly, I accepted the offer. He asked me to come with him in his house alone. Joshua was left behind.

Figure 33. A government employee is my customer: Part 3

Michael lives with his sister and nephews so we just did it in the stairs of their house. I wanted to finish it as much as possible. I took off my pants and let him do the work. It felt some pleasure in some ways but, on the other hand, sad because I realized I was doing it just for the sake of money. It took him five minutes doing oral sex with me.

Figure 34. A government employee is my customer, part 4

As soon as we finish, he gave me the P50.00 pesos. He told me to do it again should I have time. I felt good afterwards because I already had the money and I could play games with Joshua. It was not the only time it happened with the government employee. Honestly, I went back to him several times and even until now he is still my regular costumer. I also did anal sex with him once. I started to practice safe sex when I turned 14.

"A Poor Old Man Can Provide Money for Sex"

Figure 35. A poor old man can provide money for sex, part 1

It was 2:00 in the morning along Zamora St. My friend, Aaron, and I were looking for means to earn money to buy rugby and food because we were hungry. At 14, I had already become addicted to sniffing solvent.

Figure 36. A poor old man can provide money for sex: Part 2

Suddenly, an old man called us. He was 50 years old and looked very old. He offered me P80.00 pesos to have sex with him. Aaron pushed me to take the offer so we can buy rugby and food. I was hesitant but I accepted because the amount was not bad back then.

Figure 37.   A poor old man can provide money for sex: Part 3

We went to the dark alley of Zamora Street near Plaza Morga and went inside a parked jeepney. He took out off his clothes so I decided to take off my clothes, too. He started to kiss me but I refused. There was no oral sex at that time but it was my first time to do anal sex. I didn't use condom because I have no idea about anal sex. The old man just told me to insert my private part to his anus and he put saliva on it. It was disgusting. I was so ashamed with what I was doing with the old man.

Figure 38. A poor old man can provide money for sex: Part 4

After the anal sex, he gave me the money amounting to P80.00 pesos. I immediately went to Recto to purchase rugby together with Aaron. Once again, this old man became my regular client until now. We had sex for more than five times I think. Sometimes, he gives me P50.00 pesos because he is also a street dweller living along the sidewalks of Zamora Street.

A Desperate Young Girl"

Figure 39. A desperate young girl: Part 1

It was 9:00 in the evening when Michael and I decided to look for means of income along Plaza Morga. We were both 16 years old. We needed money to buy solvent and marijuana. Using drugs can make us feel we belong with my friends despite my dislike for it.

Figure 40. A desperate young girl: Part 2

We saw Arianne who is a 12-year old girl. I knew she had a big crush on me so we took advantage of it by asking her money. She was also sniffing glue at that time. She agreed to give us money in exchange for sex. She wanted to have sex with me and Michael. So, Michael offered his small shanty house along Coral Street where the job was done. Her Mother was fast asleep so we went to their bathroom with the lights off.

Figure 41. Desperate Young Girl: Part 3

I was high because of solvent that night and felt numb. It was a 30- minute sex with Arianne together with Michael. We did sexual intercourse without using any condoms. It felt good. Arianne was so silent and in pain because of what we did but she said she enjoyed it.

Figure 42. Desperate Young Girl: Part 4

After having sex with her, she gave us P20.00 which we used to buy solvent. Despite the meager amount, I was happy because she was still very young and gave us pleasure at the same time.

"My Girlfriend or My Customer?"

Figure 43. My Girlfriend or My Customer? Part 1

There was small carnival installed along Plaza Morga. Alpha and I played there. I was 16 years old and still enjoy playing games and earning prizes.

Figure 44. My Girlfriend or My Customer? Part 2

I saw my girlfriend named Cristal in the Carnival. She was a 12-year old girl who is also engaged in prostitution. I invited her to have sex with me and asked her money so I can play more in the Carnival. She agreed. We went to "Cocoy's Kainan" in Sta. Maria Street.

Figure 45. My girlfriend or my customer? Part 3

We put a used box in the street. There were also many people in there but we used blanket to cover ourselves. I took off her clothes because I was full of lust that time. Cristal enjoyed it and I had pleasure all the time.

Figure 46. My girlfriend or customer? Part 4

She gave me P400 pesos afterwards. Whenever she earns from prostitution, she gives me money. She asked me to stop doing my vices and focus on my health. I was happy to meet her especially when she introduced me to her Mother.

"Gambling Gambles My Life"

Figure 47. Gambling gambles my life: Part 1

Kenneth, my 15-year old friend and I, 16, just lost in gambling so we sniffed solvent. It was 5:00 in the morning.

Figure 48. Gambling gambles my life: Part 2

Suddenly, we found Riona, a 24-year-old gay. He was drunk. He knew I was a prostitute. He asked me to have sex with him with an offer of P100.00 pesos. Since we lost in gambling, I needed money badly.

Figure 49. Gambling gambles my life: Part 3

She invited me to the dark alley of Zamora Street behind the truck. There were a lot of gays there. It took us 10 minutes doing anal sex. I felt numb and high during this time. I didn't find it pleasurable so I told him that I was already done even though I was not.

Figure 50. Gambling gambles my life: Part 4

After having sex with Riona, she immediately gave the P100.00 pesos. I was happy. When I received the money, I went to see Kenneth to continue the gambling. We lost again.

So many bad things happened to me since I became friends with my peers. I became a theft. I knew I risking my life doing things that could lead me to death. Anyhow, I didn't believe in justice because I was beaten by the police in our community when I was 14 years old. They accused me of selling solvent along the street which I never did. This made me believe how injustice our world is. The only person who can protect ourselves is us.

I usually remain silent with my parents for the things I was doing. They never knew I was engaged in prostitution and addicted to some vices such as alcohol, cigarette, marijuana and solvent. They didn't know I was also a theft along Recto who was taking gold earrings just to sustain my vices.

The government and the community can help me by showing that they put action to their promises. All I wanted was to see consistency and justice in the implementation of their programs. Homeless people need house; but still injustice exists even in choosing people who will be granted this privilege. Some who don't even deserve are granted because they have connections. The high cost of electricity and water bills push us to do illegal acts. The gap between the rich and the poor widens. The poor even become poorer while rich become richer. These difficulties push us to strive harder to earn. The limited opportunities for poor people like us make us believe there is no hope for us and chances for a better future grow dim.

My experiences made me realize that the vices that I thought would make me feel good were a cause for regret. Being a prostituted child is difficult. I learned that money is not everything. In fact, it can destroy one's life. Doing things that don't feel good but provides pleasure to others are not beneficial. Also, stealing things only result to bad consequences.

It cannot be a means to solving problems. It often leads one to hold the railings of jail and away from love ones."

"Marlon"
"An independent child with hopeless childhood"

"Just call me Marlon. I am into several vices like solvent, alcohol and cigarettes. I am 16 years old, living in the street along Tondo, Manila. We are original settlers from the province of Bicol. We went to Manila last 2008 for my parents to earn more money in the urban city. I have no formal education, but I can read and write because my older siblings taught me. I am friendly in the community and I respect authority figures. My father died on the day I was born so I have no idea who he is.

Currently, my mother has a live-in partner who is my step-father. I have a total of 6 step-siblings because I'm the only son of my biological father. My step-father, named Rudy, has a small house made of tarpaulin along the street and works as a scavenger while my mother works as vendor of "kakanin" in Divisoria. I live independently in the street because Rudy hurts me a lot. He also steals money from my mother. I hate seeing it so I decided to live alone with my peers for almost 3 years now.

I want to pursue further education and become a teacher someday. I want to teach children who cannot provide their educational needs because I understand their situation. But, my mother doesn't support it. So, it's useless to study because I'm going to end up as a scavenger like my step-father.

I sleep in Plaza Morga together with my peers. I learned different vices and became addicted to solvent. I learned how to beg along the street to sustain my vices. It is very difficult because sometimes people in the community tease me. I get angry when I have no money. Therefore, I have no choice but to engage in prostitution because my peers are also doing it to gays.

Despite lack of support by my mother for my educational needs, we have good relationship. I know she loves me because even though she lives with my step-father, she still gives me money for my food. My auntie also teaches me to read and write and sometimes she also gives me money for food. My auntie also teaches me not to do something wrong especially saying bad words towards others.

I grew up in Bicol together with my grandparents. My grandmother takes care of me especially when I am sick and when someone bullies me. Sometimes she hurts me when I do something wrong. Because of that, I learn from my mistakes. She died last 2008. When she died, I had no choice but to live with my mother in Manila. Had my grandmother been alive, I would probably not have experienced unfortunate events including vices.

Jeffrey is one of my friends in the community. He gives me food when I am hungry. Sometimes, he lends me his things like clothes. He also gives me money to buy solvent and cigarettes. I feel protected with him because whenver I encounter petty fights on the street, he is always there to fight for me.

Marvin and Robert are always with me when I engage in prostitution. They also teenagers like me. They are the ones who deal or transact with costumers. Sometimes, my friend Joel refers gay customers who want pleasures.

I've been engaged in prostitution since I was 13 years old. This is my journey.

"Vices Pushed Me to Miserable Darkness"

Figure 51. Vices pushed me to miserable darkness: Part 1

Since I started living on the street, my life was already ruined. I learned different vices that affected my health and the way I think about the world. When I was 13 years old, we played and sniffed glue together with my friend Jordan (13 years old) and June (16 years old). We also played hide and seek. It was around 9:00 in the evening in Plaza Morga when a gay man named, Toto, called me.

Figure 52. Vices pushed me to miserable darkness, part 2

I knew him for almost a year because my peers knew him. I was quite hesitant to entertain him but still I tried. He asked me to eat with him in Tapsilogan. While eating dinner with him, he asked me to come with him in the dark alley besides the Mary Johnson Hospital and offered me 150 pesos in exchange of sex. Since I was high on that time and I needed money, I accepted his offer even though I didn't have any idea what we will do.

Figure 53. Vices push me to miserable darkness: Part 3

We went to the dark alley and asked me to take off my shorts. After taking it off, he started to do oral sex with me. It was too dark in that alley and I can't even see what he was doing. I feel pleasurable and disgusted at the same time. It's my first time so I don't have no idea what I feel.

Figure 54. Vices pushed me to miserable darkness: Part 4

After doing oral sex with me, he gave me the money worth P150 pesos and asked me to leave first. I said, 'thank you' after receiving it. I used the money to buy solvent and cigarettes since he already treated me to dinner. I did not have to buy food that time. While sniffing glue, I started to reflect what happened to me. I felt confused and motivated to do it again rather than beg on the street. I asked my friends and shared my experiences with them and I was shocked because they also doing it for gays to earn money.

I continue engaging in prostitution because I became addicted to my vices. Earning through begging is not enough to provide my needs and wants. I usually had customers just by being a bystander in the corners of Plaza Morga.

"Black-Out: An Opportunity for Gays"

Figure 55. Black out - an opportunity for gay: Part 1

It was around 8:00 in the evening. I was sitting on a bench at Plaza Morga. I was waiting for my friends who bought solvent from Isetan. I was 13 years old during that time.

Figure 56. Black out: An opportunity for gays: Part 2

Suddenly, a gay named Jennika who is 25 years old asked me if I could have sex with him. Since I already had experience having sex with gays and I needed money badly for my vices, I accepted his invitation.

Figure 57. Black out: An Opportunity for gays: Part 3

A black-out happened during this time, so it was very dark in the street. We went to the Sto. Nino Church and started having sex with him beside the stairs. It was dark and no one noticed us. Jennika offered me P200 pesos if I could have anal sex with him. I agreed and he taught me how to do it. He held my penis and inserted it to his anus. He asked me to do it faster and harder and it felt very much with pleasure. I was confused because I had no idea that penis can be inserted into the anus.

Figure 58. Black out, an Opportunity for gays: Part 4

After 20 minutes of sexual act, he told me that he had fun and enjoyed what I did. He gave me the P200 pesos and went back to Plaza Morga. I was happy upon receiving the money because I can buy more solvent and cigarettes. I invited my peers to buy 'Emeperador' lights. I was drunk that night.

"A Regular Costumer Who Became a Friend"

Figure 59. A regular customer who became a friend: Part 1

It was around 4:00 in the afternoon in Plaza Morga when Toto (29 years old) invited me to come with him to roam around the community. He had a motorcycle and asked me to join him in his trip. I was so hungry during that time so I decided to come with him expecting he would feed me. I treated Toto as my parent because I got support from him. While we were roaming in the community using his motorcycle, we had a stop-over and bought drinks and snacks.

Figure 60. A regular customer who became a friend: Part 2

We bought soft drinks and fudge bar in one of the mini-stores in Wagas St., Tondo Manila. We had a conversation. He shared his life experiences with me. He told me his hardships and difficulties in life and why he became a gay. I pitied him and I was sad knowing his story. After the conversation, he asked me to have sex with him in the dark alley of Wagas. It was already 6:00 in the evening and dark. Since I needed money badly, I accepted his offer.

Figure 61. A regular customer who became a friend: Part 3

We went to the dark alley of the street and he started to remove my shorts. He licked my penis and did oral sex with me. Suddenly, there were two gays who saw us but Toto continued what he was doing while the two gays continued watching. I was afraid because they might join us. We had sex for 40 minutes and the two gays stayed there until we were finished.

After having sex with him, he immediately gave me P100 pesos and abandoned me not saying a word. The two gays saw me receiving money from Toto but I ignored them. I was happy because I had money and went to a canteen and ate my dinner. After eating, I bought solvent together with my friends.

My Vices made Me Numb

Figure 62. My vices made me numb: Part 1

When I was 16, I usually hang out with my friends in the different alleys of Tondo. Suddenly, my friend named Pards, who is 13 years old, also engaged in prostitution, saw a gay customer. We just finished sniffing glue that time but we still needed money to buy a new bottle. I was not hesitant to ask money from the gay so we went to meet him.

Figure 63. My vices made me numb: Part 2

He introduced himself as Joan. He was a 24-year old gay selling vegetables in Divisoria. He asked me and Pards to eat dinner with him, in which we agreed to join him. We went to "JOJO'S CAFETERIA" along Herbosa Street. After taking dinner, Joan whispered to my ear asking me to come with him in the dark alley. I thought that he will just be asking a companion. I had no idea what he was planning.

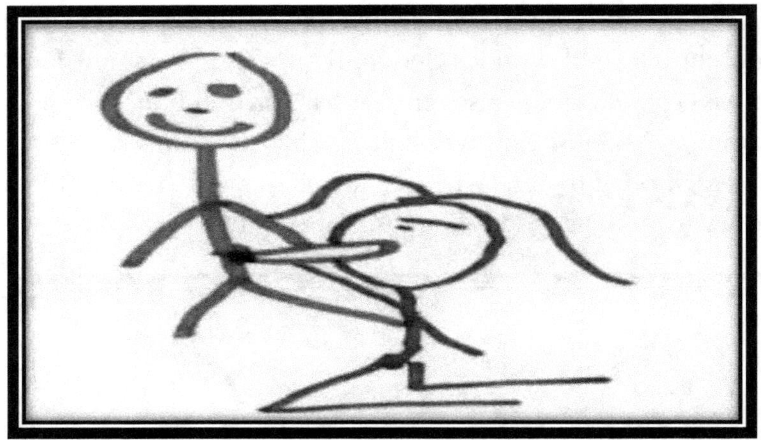

Figure 65. My vices made me numb: Part 3

When we reached the nearest dark alley where we took dinner, he offered me P300 pesos in exchange for sex. I was excited because it was a lot of money; so, I said yes. He started to take off my shorts and did oral sex with me. It was around 11:00 in the evening. It was very dark in the alley so no one noticed us. I was feeling numb and I didn't know what we did in that alley. I was so high because we just sniffed a lot of glue that time. I think our sex lasted 50 minutes.

Figure 64. My vices made me numb: Part 4

After having sex with Joan, he gave the P300 pesos. I tried looking for Pards. Joan told me that it was all the money he had and expressed gratitude to him by saying 'thank you.' We separate ways. Pards and I bought drugs in Kapulong Highway worth around P100-P150 pesos. We knew a lot of people where we can buy.

I had a good relationship with my mother. Even if I ran away from home, she took time to visit me in the street to give me money for my food. Sometimes, I felt so ashamed to the community especially when someone sees me sniffing glue. I felt like they were judging me as a bad person.

All I needed was an opportunity to have a noble work. I wanted to help my mother to earn a living. I wanted to have a noble job even if it was difficult. I realized it was very difficult earning money if you are uneducated. The opportunity to look for a job and have a better future is limited."

"Pat"
"A boy trapped to engage in prostitution to survive"

"You can call me Pat. I am 17 years old staying in the different streets of Manila. At first, I thought we had a great life. I grew up in a small shanty house together my parents. When I turned 10, my father died. He committed suicide. He hanged himself in front of me telling he was giving up life because he had no work while my mother was getting addicted to drugs. At my very young age, I became independent. I took care of myself. Since my father died, we did not have money to continue renting our house. So, we decided to live in the street. We have relatives in Manila but they refuse to help us because they hate my mother.

Living in the street was very difficult. I had to adjust to a lot of things including getting along with gangs to be safe and protected. If I was not going to do this, I might risk my life just to live. The problem was that I chose wrong peers whose influence was all negative such as smoking, drinking alcohol and drugs.

I met Ashley, Eugene and Robin. We were all minors who protected one another. Because of them, I started neglecting my mother including myself.

My mother became more addicted to various drugs. Hence, I became freer. I can do anything I wanted. Currently, she has a live-in partner who is already old and has a psychological disorder. She only uses the man for the sake of money because he has pension. My peers also influenced me to stop schooling. After all, I was no longer interested pursuing my studies. I could not find a reason to continue studying since my mother did not support me. Despite my desire to pursue tertiary education to take up Information Technology, I guess it was impossible because it was still a long way to go. I only finished primary education and had difficulty reading and writing.

Since I was living in the street, I became vulnerable from abuse. My life was totally ruined when I met a gay stranger.

"Innocence Turned Weakness"

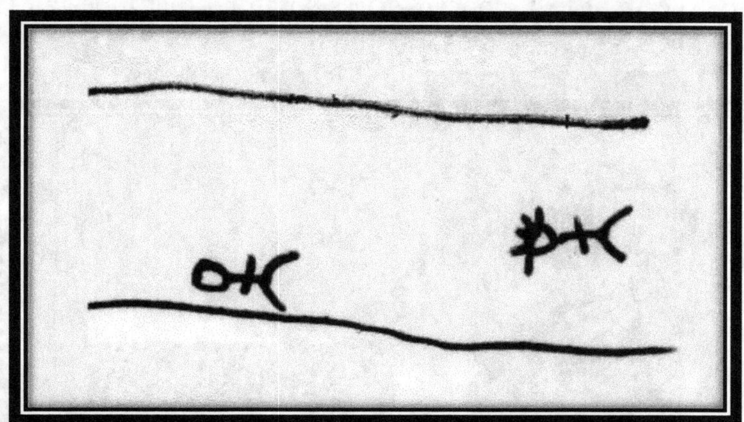

Figure 66. Innocence turned weakness: Part 1

He was a 24-year old gay. I had no idea what his motives were when he called me. I was 12 years old that time and he asked me if I wanted money. I replied, "yes" knowing I needed it badly since I haven't eaten any meals that day.

Figure 67. Innocence turned weakness: Part 2

He offered me P200.00 just to come with him in his house. We went to Caloocan. I was so afraid that time but he looked nice so I agreed to come with him.

Figure   68. Innocence turned weakness: Part 3

When we were in his house in Caloocan, he asked me to take off my clothes. I was totally scared and asked him why. He told me that I needed money so the only way to give me the P200.00 pesos was to have sex with him. I was shocked because I had no idea about sex especially with a gay. He instructed me what to do. He did oral sex. I was confused and disgusted. I hated what happened.

Figure 69. Innocence turned weakness: Part 4

I didn't feel any pleasure when he was doing it. After the act, he gave me the P200.00 pesos. I cried all the way home because I felt so ashamed having done it. I remained silent and didn't tell my Mother about it because I was afraid she might hurt me.

Every night after the incident, I kept thinking what the reason behind everything was. I realized that it could be the best way to earn money so that I can provide for my own needs. So I tried to look for a gay to offer my body. With my different experiences, I realized that not all gays and customers are the same.   Not every gay is generous. There are gays who take advantage and are mean.

At the age of 12, I started working to provide for my own meals. Sometimes, I asked money from my mother but still it was insufficient and not enough to buy a meal. I needed to exert more effort to live. I even tried to look for a job like carpentry, "kargador," dishwasher, helper, baby sitter, and even janitorial. The problem though was the bad treatment I received from people in these industries. The treated me like a slave. It hurt my feelings. I realized that it was more difficult compared to lying in bed having sex with someone and getting paid.

I found out that my peers also engaged in prostitution had similar experiences. According to them it was the usual business in the community. So I asked information what should be the proper way to do the transaction and what I can do. They taught me things like having a conversation and even taught me the 'how' to steal their things after having sex. We usually watched porn movies in the internet café to know different positions and actions if we have a customer. We had no pimps. We earned money for ourselves. We used it for food, vices and drugs.

Five years as a child prostitute, honestly, I don't know how many customers I had. All I know is that there were a lot and it gave me an average of P200 to P500 pesos as earning. Sometimes I found it pleasurable if they are clean and looks good but sometimes I get disappointed and disgusted if they're ugly and old. I usually find my customers in Plaza Morga and

Isetan Recto Malls. I had an experience having sex in dark alleys, movie houses, motels, hotels and even in the comfort room of the malls. Sex can happen anywhere if you find ways. I'm doing this to live not to die. With everything that happened to me, I learned not to trust any people around me. I became numb and I felt hopeless. I am ashamed with what I've done and how I destroyed my life totally. Because of these experiences, I became independent. Somehow, I can live alone. If I don't do this kind of job, I will be nothing. I have limited skills and no one cares. This is the easy way to earn money. I know it could affect my health, but that is life. There will be death at least not the way how my father died.

I tried to change but failed. I took Accreditation and Equivalency Exam hoping to pass the secondary examination so I can pursue my dream, but failed. A lot of people tried to help me – social workers, friends and even the church. However, how can their words of encouragement, advice and lunch meals do to a hopeless life like mine? At the end of the day, I need to survive in this cruel reality called life. Honestly, prostitution is my world and I guess I will never stop unless I die.

What I can I recommend to the government to make children like us feel safe in this world? If there are easy but legal job opportunities for independent children like me to sustain our basic needs, that will be enough to end this phenomenon. If the government can provide us ways to contribute to the society and hear our voices by investigating deeper the real status of children in the street, they can provide immediate action to address the situation. If educated people and people in authority would treat us fairly and just, it will be a good start for us.

Engaging prostitution is not even a choice; it is one way to live and survive in this world for children like me who live in it.

CHAPTER 2

THE MEANING OF THEIR EXPERIENCES

Fitting-in with Peers for acceptance and protection

Social rejection happens when one individual is purposely excluded from social situation. Humans are social creatures by nature and rejection is almost always emotionally painful. Some rejection in life is normal and just about everyone has experienced or will experience, some sort of social exclusion during his lifetime. But from my co-researcher's experiences, the rejection is much more devastating because they already repeatedly rejected by the community.

Fitting-in with a certain group is extremely important. Based on the social facts gathered from my co-researchers, peer influence isn't all bad. It shows that among peers they can find friendship and acceptance and able to share their experiences that can build lasting bonds. These peers listen and give them feedback as they try out new ideas, explore beliefs and discuss their problems.

Peers can help them in decision making, gives opportunities to try out new social skills, encourage them to fight to live. Accordingly, their friendship has inevitable ups and downs. Yet the feeling of satisfaction and security that derive from their interaction with their peers outweigh periodic problems. My co-researchers developed little faith in their own abilities to achieve interpersonal goals and, thus, are easily overwhelmed by their normal ups and downs of social interaction.

Finally, my co-researchers suffer from painful feeling of isolation. In their search for a sense of group belonging, they become vulnerable to the influence of delinquent and child prostitution.

Influenced by Peers Engaged in Prostitution

The peers of my co-researchers made them become less dependent on their family. It exposes them to knowledge to which they have no access to their family. It affects my co-researchers the way they think and perceive the reality. I observed that peer group influence has a bearing on prostitution, and loss of cultural values for dignity of human life.

Based on the social facts gathered, my co-researchers are influenced by their peers and motivated to live in the street and entertain gay strangers to earn a living in the community. The prevalence of prostituted children has become a serious problem to the Government and society in general. This is because oftentimes my co-researchers move to the streets in search of costumers.

It is generally believed that boys who engage in prostitution not only endanger and destroy their bodies but also spoil the image of the country.

Low standard of living has more tendencies for them to engage in prostitution that's why it's important that parents should give them proper upbringing and necessary financial provisions so that they will not look for alternative ways to make up for their shortfalls and hence, predisposed to prostitution tendencies. Their parents should monitor the type of peers or be-friends their children keep, or must check the types of attitude being exhibited by then before their children because adults are seen by children as social pillars and should be taught right values, morals, attitudes, and behavior of life.

God Exists and always Blessed Us

I've learned to allow feeling abandoned, unheard and ignored by God. My obligation as a Christ-follower is not to pretend that negative feelings don't exist. We all know they do. The prophets and disciples get angry with God often, and they let Him know it. God prefers our emotionally fidelity to the Sunday School Sunshine façade we've learned to display. He wants us to tell Him how we really feel. The Bible tells us to weep with those who weep. Doesn't that imply many will have real, legit reasons to weep? Doesn't that almost ensure some problems will go unsolved? Christians, then, shouldn't ignore the real emotions we feel in moments of tragedy and loss. We should face them, together.

Despite His silence, God is not happy with our problems. He does not sit on a bejeweled throne with an air of indifference to our problems. I picture him with looking down on us through sad, pain-filled, eyes. I picture a God who, at minimum, weeps with us. God is not smiling at dying children, rape, murder, poverty, disease, and depression.

God is all-powerful, meaning He can accomplish anything that can be accomplished with power. He cannot use power to do "non-power" kinds of things, such as the logically impossible. He cannot make two plus two equal five, violate His unchangeable nature, make Himself go out of existence and come back into existence, and He cannot make morally responsible persons without allowing for the possibility of those persons making wrong choices. The Bible says that suffering is the consequence of the wrong choice (sin) of morally responsible persons. If God always prevented people from sinning, or always prevented the consequences of sin, then human goodness would be mere programming, not true goodness. We do not pat a computer on its back when it executes its program -- it is a determined function, not an exercise of moral responsibility. Suffering, the consequence of human sin, is not caused by God, but by the sin of persons with moral responsibility. Also, God has not abandoned the world to eternally suffer the consequences of sin. He sent His Son, Jesus Christ, to provide ultimate freedom from the consequences of sin. It is wrong to indict God because suffering is not yet eliminated, just as it would be wrong to indict a doctor who treats a gunshot wound he didn't cause, simply because the wound is not healed instantly.

Our assurance that God will eliminate suffering is not the only comfort God gives us. While God did not cause suffering, he has given it purpose. It became the vehicle for our salvation when "Jesus, the author and perfecter of our faith, who for the joy set before him endured the cross, scorning its shame" (Hebrews 12:2). Complete avoidance of suffering is not an option for any of us. Our option is to waste our experience or realize God's purposes amid suffering. Through suffering we can learn patience, self-discipline, trust, and many other "virtues."

When we suffer, we can experience the love, compassion, and self-denial of those who help us. When we help someone, who is suffering, we find significance in our own lives as well.

Not all pain is "bad" in the moral sense. God created us with nerve endings that use pain to protect us. Pain keeps us from burning our hands in a campfire, bending our legs back until the joint breaks, neglecting nourishment until we starve, etc. Suffering can also be a direct, just consequence of our own actions. Our sense of justice says that it is "good" when an exploiter loses his friends, even though loneliness is "painful." It is good when a mugger is locked up, even though he "suffers" the loss of his freedom.

All humans have a moral conscience, even corrupted by sin and often ignored. Our conscience should not rejoice in sin, suffering, and death. When we see innocents suffering, we should experience moral outrage and seek to rescue the sufferer. When we see someone suffer death, we should experience loss and sorrow. Sin, suffering, and death are not the destinies for which God created us. He created us to enjoy perfect, good, loving fellowship with Him for eternity. Despite our moral betrayal, he continues to offer eternal life.

We do not like to be prostituted but had no choice

Prostitution is often described as a "victimless crime," or a "consensual crime" because in theory, no one present at the crime is unwilling. It is a myth. Certainly, male child prostitution is a particularly lethal form of violence against children, and a violation of a child's most basic human rights.

Sadly, majority of my co-researchers entered prostitution before they even reach the age of consent. In other words, their first commercial sexual interactions are rape. In this study, it indicates that most of my co-researchers were sexually and physically-abused.

Another myth is that most boys choose to enter the sex industry. Again, while this is true for a small number of sex workers, the research indicates that for most my co-researchers, it is a highly constrained choice. Ultimately, viewing prostitution as a genuine "choice" for them, such as janitorial, and waiter which diminishes the possibility of getting them out and improving their lives.

In fact, all my co-researchers wanted to opt out but they lack viable alternatives. They are unable to leave because of addiction or need to feed their family. The misconception that this is a choice makes outsiders less likely to help them from getting much needed help, and it also shapes the way they think about themselves.

I believe when our culture and society exchange judgment for compassion, healing can come to thousands of young boys in the Philippines, which they will feel protected, loved and cared by the society.

Taking the Risk Alone to survive amidst a difficult Life

Leaving home at an early age forced my co-researchers to decide prematurely with whom to rely for survival. Since most of them cannot depend on parental or familial assistance their options are limited. They are forced to pursue child prostitution and use their internal strengths to navigate this often precarious and hazardous street environment.

Some service providers and society in general view homeless young children on a one-dimensional level as victims, emphasizing the maltreatment, substance abuse, and poverty that lead to their precocious disengagement from the family. Although these viewpoints have merit, depicting homeless children only as victims may advance the notion that they have diminished skills and capacities. Therefore, this study identifies various aspects of fortitude that allow them to survive and succeed in homeless lifestyles. Homelessness clearly requires problem-solving skills and resilience often ignored in more problem-oriented research and service provision. By encouraging my co-researchers to discuss their opinions, feelings, and perspectives, the strengths they had developed to survive their hostile environments became evident.

Developing street smarts appear necessary to live within the street economy and function in spite of adversity and often unsafe and harsh conditions. My co-researchers develop subsistence skills and knowledge required to survive. Because of their experiences, they often offer support and assistance to less experienced peers; however, individuals are expected to be independent and self-sustaining. Little respect is given to those with limited street smarts or those who remain connected to traditional sources of support, demonstrating these children's conviction concerning the significance of independence and its role in homelessness. Gaining experience on the street significantly shapes my co-researchers behaviors and perceptions.

My co-researchers infrequently acknowledged and recognized their own internal and external strengths. Only when asked specifically about their skills did they appear to identify their own individual competencies. When elicited, however, they did note that a positive attitude was needed to survive day-to-day, and they viewed their own intelligence and ability to interact with others as skills they had developed and used to get along. These boys felt they were caring for themselves better than others could or had done previously.

Peer Pressure Influence Negative Behavior and Addiction

Peer pressure is the influenced of a group that encourages young boys to change their attitudes, behavior and values for them to be fully accepted in their group. It is very common to my co-researchers because they are the ones who spend more time with their friends in the street. Most of my co re-searchers are afraid to be alone so they search for a group of people that they can be with or they can rely on. Peer pressure can be positive or negative but mostly it is negative according to their social facts. Peer pressure is portrayed as negative and had bad effects on their lives. The negative effects of peer pressure include the following based on the gathered social facts: theft, computer games addiction, bullying, disrespect elders, solvent, losing interest in school, possibility of addiction to prohibited drugs, smoking and alcoholic drinks.

They do it because of their friends are doing it and they think that is the way to be "fit in" the group they wanted to join. It can ruin their lives and their relationship with other people. Their friends will push them to use drugs or drink alcoholic drinks for them to be accepted in the group. Since they become addicted in those things, it shows that it affected their studies, health andtheir lives.

It is true that we can't live alone or we can't live without friends. But it is our choice to be in a right path. We should choose the people who can be trusted and will give us good influence. We should be strong enough to say no if someone's asking us to do bad things. My co-researcher should be independent enough and they should be responsible. They should always have self-discipline. We are the ones who make our life so we should be wise enough in making decisions. We should make the right decision in our lives so that we can have a successful life in the future.

Most of my co-researchers became dependent on their vices. This addiction can be a positive factor on one's life, if we realize that it may be the one thing that enables one to endure the very worst situations and go on to live a life that can later be full and rewarding. It is how the addiction is addressed and dealt with that will determine how they will fare later life. Addiction may have been the tool that has kept their feelings and memories at bay. Recovery is not a straight incline leading directly to a desired goal, but it does follow a somewhat predictable path. To get on this path, they must first recognize their problem and can address their addictive behavior, and then must understand the role that the addiction has served. They must learn the value of themselves person, rather than as a sexual object. By doing this, they will understand that recovery is not possible without abstaining from it. By doing this they can develop a new sense of themselves. They begin to appreciate their sense of strength and purpose. They begin to take responsibility for their own lives and happiness. Then a new way of looking at life emerges.

Ashamed of Myself and the Community

As humans, we are social animals. One consequence of this is the potential to be uncomfortable or anxious around other people. My co re-searchers tend to be more inhibited and fearful around people they don't know well. If only these children are adequately encouraged and supported when they are young, they will outgrow their anxiousness.

My co-researchers had difficult time in life for self-consciousness and discomfort with oneself. How well does one fit into a peer group is of great importance and affects their growing sense of self. If only it all goes well, they will grow into a self-confident and mature adult.

At their very young age, they develop anxiety. They encounter new stresses that lack adequate coping skills to deal with. Severe anxiety states develop, along with the fear of because they notice that anxiety. My co-researchers developed social anxiety, which is characterized by fears of feeling embarrassed or humiliated around other people. Underlying this is the fear of being seen as weak, defective, or somehow not okay in the eyes of other people. Underlying this fear is shame.

Shame is a feeling of being flawed or unacceptable in some way. Sometimes this feeling is very vague, especially to my co-researchers because they don't know where their discomfort is coming from. As I reflect, guilt is the experience that you made a mistake, while shame is the experience that you are a mistake.

Early in life, shaming experiences happen in one's family, in school, and among peers. Shame has the adaptive function of guiding them to conform to the ethics, morals, and rules of our environment. However, negative shameful experiences cause them to feel hopeless and inadequate, and lead to depression. Generally, there are certain areas in which they feels lacking or flawed: personal attractiveness, intelligence, competence, and lovability are common themes.

It is almost impossible to get through childhood without experiencing at least a few shaming experiences. It is helpful to be aware of one's areas of shame because shame very much influences how we interact with the world. Avoidance of meeting people is a typical response of someone with social anxiety. Dependence on alcohol and drugs may also be used to numb the anxiety. For some of my co-researchers, criticizing or ridiculing others to make one feel less inferior is another strategy. Clearly, these strategies can have very negative consequences in one's life.

We're all on our own journeys, celebrating our own minor and major victories and battling our own demons or insecurities or general problems that gets us down. Most of my co-researchers are doing the best they can; and some of them are even good at hiding their problems that keeps them from being the best versions of themselves. People will always be our critic, because they are missing pieces of who we are. Once we sense our own importance is the day we will be set free from everyone's judgment.

Hopelessly Regretting a Miserable Life

People with a positive attitude have a way of instilling a sense of confidence in the people around them. They have a gentle way of making people feel that everything will be alright, no matter the threatening storm. They always seem to know something that others do not and the truth be told, they do. Positive minded people always know that every storm can be calmed; they have confidence that a solution is within reach, they know that every challenge can be turned into an opportunity. It is for this reason that you will rarely hear a positive minded person complaining about a situation they are facing. The reason they do not complain is because when faced with a crisis, they do not see the crisis, but an opportunity, so how can they complain about an opportunity?

Every storm that we experience is an opportunity to grow. The greatest challenges that my co-researcher's experiences, is not a problem of being illiterate but those who are not able to relearn and unlearn. The biggest teacher in life is challenges; it provides us with greater learning experiences, especially those that we overcame. Perhaps one the good reasons why we never forget what we went through in life, those personal experiences remain vivid in our minds. That is how powerful our minds are, nothing can erase what we experience. It has been said, it is difficult to appreciate the mountain top, if you have not been through the valley lows. Remember that it is not what happens to you that is important but your response to that negative situation will determine the outcome.

I am not denying the fact that there are also many people who went through difficult experiences but later forget what they went through. As a result, many of them continue to experience the same challenge over again. They keep making the same mistakes and end experiencing the same consequences, they keep going through pain and disappointments. This simply indicates that they did not pick up any lesson from their storms. When we refuse to learn from our dark periods in lives, we always never grow out what we learnt from those storms.

Innocent Children are Vulnerable

As a society, we often seem to care more about protecting our cultural ideal of childhood innocence than about meeting the actual or real needs of children—especially commercially and sexually-exploited children. To fit the ideal of purity, children require high levels of social capital; preferably, they're white, belong to the middle or upper class, and heterosexual. They have limited or no sexual experience, they enjoy secure health care, housing, and education, and they live within a supportive nuclear family. In my experience, children living without access to such resources are too often labelled "bad kids" and blamed for "choosing" to exist outside of this ideal.

Prostituted child is, perhaps, the most distressing form of child abuse. The innocence of a childhood shattered, causing a deep feeling of shame, poisoning the sense of self and excluding the child from education, friends and the broader society. Children don't yet have well-developed boundaries and a sense of self. They have difficulty understanding the powerful feelings often involved with sexual sharing, the natural right they have to the privacy of their own bodies, and the right they have to say "no" to any touching which feels uncomfortable or invasive. For these reasons, a child can be an easy and vulnerable target for a sexual predator or other sexually confused adult who has not developed their own appropriate boundaries and sense of morality.

No child enters prostitution when they have a choice. Prostitution is viewed as a social ill that is unaccepted, prohibited and fought in most parts of our continent. Prostitution is not only a question of morality but a human problem, a problem of human exploitation, a problem of societal failure in providing equal opportunities. At the end, no boys would like to be a prostitute but the problems force them to be in such a situation. The circumstances that lead these young boys away from their games and innocence of childhood and what should be, the love and gentle kindness of their family, into the shadows of prostitution, may vary and circumstances differ, suffering though is common to all those forced into such a lifestyle, the impact long lasting and severe, the consequences dire, destroying many lives.

They often internalize that they are to blame for their desperate situations. The dearth of safe housing and economic opportunity furthers the isolation. Unfortunately, exploiters know that vulnerable children have few choices and manipulate them by promising that they will fill the voids of missing love, protection, and basic needs like food, clothing, and shelter.

A Loving Family that Provides Basic Needs

It's no stretch to say that a person has a serious advantage in life if they come from a loving, supportive home. Many people still succeed even if they come from less-than-ideal family situations, but having our basic needs met, knowing that our parents love us and learning life lessons at home make all the challenges of day-to-day living that much easier to face. Likely, as an adult you want a happy home for your family.

For any parent who has children, their main role is to care for and prepare their child for independent survival as an adult. We all begin completely dependent on our parents, and so if they raise us successfully, we leave as self-respecting and self-responsible adults. We are then able to confidently face and cope with the challenges of life.

Of course, not all co-researchers are the same, as we each have differing levels of confidence, optimism, self-esteem and self-worth. Each of these characteristics are greatly influenced by how a child was raised and the type of parents that raised them.

In general, it can be said that there are two main types of parents based on the gathered social facts. The first are those who treat their children with love and respect. These types of parents are likely to produce children that grow up having the highest levels of self-esteem and confidence. The second types of parents are those who treat children without love and respect, and these children are likely to grow up having the lowest levels of self-esteem and confidence.

However, things are not quite as simple or straightforward as has just been described. A parent may treat their child with love and respect but do it in the wrong way. This may then result in a child who has low level of self-esteem and confidence when one would have expected the opposite to happen. I realize that it is important to remember that childhood development can be influenced not only by what parent does for their child, but crucially, how they do it.

This is no coincidence. God organizes us into families so that we can grow up in happiness and safety, and so that we can learn to love others selflessly—the key to true joy. Within the family is the best place to learn to love others the way Heavenly Father loves each one of us.

Escaping Through Silence for Peace

Based on the narratives from my co-researchers, runaways have provided new evidence that physical and sexual abuse are important contributors not only to chronic runaway behavior, but also to delinquency and emotional difficulties.

There are many understandable reasons why a prostituted child is not likely to tell anyone about their situation. Often, their previous costumers will convince the child that they won't be believed or that they are somehow responsible for the abuse and will be punished for it. My co-researchers may care about or feel protective from their costumers and may feel they'd be betraying this person by telling about the sexual contact and they may use this information to help maintain the secrecy. Some of my co-researchers frequently remain silent to protect a non-abusive parent from upsetting information.

Humiliation, shame and fear equal silence. These emotions cause that response to my co-researchers. Offenders reinforce these feelings by the things they say and do to the prostituted child. They use the shame and fear to bind the child to them and isolate them from others who might help them. The prostituted child is left feeling alone, isolated and very different from everyone around them.

My co-researchers describe this as a surreal feeling –to see other kids leading normal lives all around them, but feel so different and separate from them due to the sexual contact they have experienced. This shame and silence can last for decades.

They are waiting until their adult hood to share their secret. For my co-researchers, the shame and secrecy is compounded by the fear that their own sexuality may have something to do with it, or at least that others will think so.

Sometimes, they may be confused if they experienced positive physical pleasure, arousal, or emotional intimacy from engaging sexual contact. This confusion can make it difficult for them to speak up. My co-researchers feel that they permitted the abuse and should have been able to stop it. Remember that there are no situations where they are responsible for any sexual interaction with a more powerful child or adult.

People who abuse my co-researchers may offer a combination of gifts or treats and threats about what will happen if the child says 'no' or tells someone. They may scare them with threats of being hurt physically, but more often the threat is about what will be lost if they tell e.g. their manhood and dignity.

To keep the prostitution in silent, the costumer will often play on the child's fear, embarrassment or guilt about what is happening, perhaps convincing them that no one will believe them or that they will be punished. Sometimes the costumer will convince the prostituted child that he enjoyed it and wanted it to happen.

Developmental Impact of Family Issues

All my co-researchers come from broken families. The family earns very little and they experience lower levels of educational achievement. Worse, they pass the prospect of meager incomes and family instability on to their children, creating a vicious cycle, if not expanding cycle, of economic distress.

Most of my co-researchers lost their father. Their father's death has long-term effects on their lives. Practically, it is traumatic for a child to witness the death of father who commits suicide in front of him just like co-researcher 6.

Certain negative effects are brought about by a father's death. When a father dies, no one can replace him, not even a mother or any other relative. The loss of a father can result to lower living standards for the bereaved children. Not only is a child emotionally-affected, without a father who is the breadwinner in a family, children may drop out of school to work especially if he is the eldest among the siblings.

My co-researchers experienced deficits in emotional development. They seem in tears and depressed with their varied experiences relative to family issues they encounter. Some of them showed very little emotional reaction to the problem of their parents; however, they were battling with negative feelings. This emotional suppression makes it hard for me to help them process their feelings in more developmental appropriate ways.

Slowed academic development is another common issue that affects my co-researchers. The emotional stress of a broken family can be enough to stunt their academic progress, but lifestyle changes and instability of a broken family can contribute to poor educational outcomes. This poor academic progress can stem from several factors, including instability in home environment, inadequate financial resources and inconsistent routines.

It also shows effects on their social relationships in several ways. First, some of my co-researchers act out their distress regarding the brokenness of their family by acting aggressive and by engaging in bullying behavior, both of which can negatively affect peer relationships. Others experienced anxiety, which can make it difficult for them to seek positive social interactions and engage in developmentally beneficial activities such as teen sports. They develop a cynical attitude toward relationships and harbor feelings of mistrust toward their parents.

By its very nature, broken family, changes not only the structure of the family but also its dynamics. Some of my co-researchers need to perform more chores and assume additional roles in the new household's basic functioning. Additionally, since most of my co-researchers are the eldest among their siblings, they take on a parental-type of role when interacting with younger siblings because of their mother's inability to be present in the way they were before the loss of their father.

Trying to Look for Means to End Prostitution

My co-researchers felt trapped between wanting the prostitution to stop and being terrified of other people knowing what has been done to them. That fear kept them silent while prostitution went on for years before it was stopped.

As an adult, I understand and view sexuality very differently from my young co-researchers. The knowledge I gained with experience and time provides me the tools to better understand an event that happens while young. It is common for prostituted children not to name their experience as abuse until they reach adulthood.

There are many reasons for a child to engage in prostitution. Some of my co-researchers stated that they were attracted to the large sum of money they can earn while they are still young. They also see themselves as a helping hand to their mothers to provide the basic need of the family.

Most of them intended to leave prostitution by trying to beg in the street to earn a living; but, despite this means, it's still insufficient to provide for their needs and wants. At the other end of the spectrum of prostitution are the street children. Most of them are addicted to drugs, and many are motivated into prostitution against their will but by their peers. Their experience of sexual abuse is a fact; more than anything else, it seems to provide the reason as to how and why some of them became prostitutes. Some of my co-researchers are addicted to drugs which resulted to the development of serious health problems like STD.

Finally, some co-researchers view prostitution as their way out of poverty. While they may choose to sell themselves, it is economic necessity that drives them. They tried to look for other means to end prostitution but unable to get jobs and are sometimes pressured because they are the only bread winners in the family.

Unsafe Community Developed Mistrust

My co-researchers invested themselves in relationships that left them deeply wounded. They've been abandoned and taken advantage of, and left with little to show for what they've given. They lost their sense of security and personal value in the process. And what's worse, they tend to either repeat the same mistakes of judgment over and over and lock the doors of their hearts entirely and throw away the key.

My co-researchers feel powerless, insecure and afraid which are the basic ingredients for depression. If I add their feeling of loneliness they won't listen to what other people tell them; if they disregard or invalidate their feelings, they have the potential to lead miserable lives as option to end their pain.

They can be discriminated against on a structural level as well as on a personal level. In other words, on a personal level they can be targeted by individuals who look at them with disgust, or even by violence, being attacked simply for being a street child. On a structural level, they get discriminated against in employment, as if they have no fixed abode. They are unable to apply for jobs; but, even if they get an interview they can be knocked back since they are living in the street and can be treated like a slave just like the experience of co-researcher 6.

They are discriminated against, inadvertently by large corporations, such as local authorities, who have procedures and protocols, but if they have not got the skills or prior knowledge of what is expected of them, such as where to access help or able to complete a form due to literacy problems, they will not receive help they need in the community.

My co-researchers have a low propensity to trust. Their propensity to trust is based on many factors, chief among them being their personality, early childhood role models and experiences, beliefs and values, culture, self-awareness and emotional maturity. The combination of these factors and experiences shapes how quickly, and how much trust they extend to others. Their experiences may have resulted in their viewing trust as something to be earned, not given, so therefore they withhold trust from others until they are sure they deserve it. Having a low propensity to trust can hold them back from experiencing true joy and fulfillment in relationships.

They also have unrealistic expectations. Unrealistic, unspoken, and unclear expectations are a primary cause for low or broken trust in relationships, and the higher the expectations the more likely it is that they won't be met. Usually, trust isn't something people openly talk about or address in relationships until it has been broken. By then, it's often too late to salvage the relationship or the breach of trust seems too big to overcome. It's much better to have the awkward or uncomfortable discussion up front about roles, responsibilities, and expectations, then, it is to deal with the fallout when either party falls short.

Lastly, past hurts hold them back. Since they have been hurt and have experienced pain, they often hurt other people in a dysfunctional form for self-protection. Whether it's unnecessarily withholding trust, having unrealistic expectations of others, being trapped in a victim mentality, lashing out at others, or operating out of low self-esteem, their past experiences with broken trust can easily derail them from developing healthy, high-trust relationships. You may not be able to control what happens to you, but you can control what happens within you.

Opportunity is a Good Start to End Prostitution

My co-researchers are aware of the need to address the gap between enactment and enforcement of laws. Aside from the need to set-up functional and efficient monitoring systems, the need to educate the public and government officials and public/civil servants about these child-focused laws and policies was also seen as critical. It was evident that public awareness and understanding within the justice system about national laws is lacking. Hence, there must be an intention to provide special protection measures for children in the spirit of the convention to counter this lack of commitment to enforce these laws.

If these prostituted children from the street can have job opportunities that are legal and appropriate for them at their young age, then that will be sufficient to provide for their basic needs. This can be a means to help them stop from engaging in prostitution. This could be extremely challenging yet very rewarding. The barriers our youth face while trying to penetrate today's market make the task so much more complicated.

If the government and other agencies could provide employment opportunities to my co-researchers, this could pave the way for stopping their engagement in prostitution. However, they may find it difficult to get a legal job because they cannot provide a stable or permanent address. Employers certainly need permanent addresses to process payroll, collect personal information and establish emergency contacts. Having no permanent address can be poorly perceived by employers and embarrassing for our youth.

They can also have emotional instability at work because they have often experienced traumatic events and great losses in their lives. These events can be accompanied by depression, low motivation and poor self-esteem. Most of them came from very unstable environments and low level of education. Most are elementary undergraduates and has difficulty reading and writing; moreover, they have very limited computer skills.

If they can work in a legal job and provided an opportunity they will have little to no appropriate clothing for job search. They also have less access to facilities to maintain their hygiene and are often unable to even get a good night sleep. It can also be a challenge to maintain their belongings for they are living in the street.

Due to the changes in our economy over the last few years, they are at an even greater disadvantage as they compete with experienced and educated adults for entry level positions. My co-researchers have been let down, heartbroken and disappointed by many of the adults in their lives. This creates a sense of hopelessness. Without the support and nurturing of caring adults, they find it hard to believe that life can be more rewarding.

CHAPTER 3

THE ESSENCE OF THEIR EXPERIENCE

Prostituted Male Street Children Seek Belongingness and Acceptance

Belonging-ness is my term for the feeling of belonging. We may say objectively, from the outside, that a person belongs to this or that group, but that person may or may not feel that connection. My co-researchers feel alienated even though their parents and teachers think they're okay; the alienation is an experience of non-belongingness. This feeling of belonging is a basic need, so it is important to appreciate some of the psychological and social dynamics involved. Based on a greater understanding, we may be more able to diagnose problems that arise out of a lack of belongingness and suggest more rationally formulated individual and social actions for promoting or restoring a sense of belonging.

This problem is more relevant today because the postmodern condition has intensified alienation. To say that our culture is postmodern is to recognize more vividly that the changes in culture in the last several decades has made life qualitatively different from fifty years ago (the mid-20th century being the mid-late point of modernity). Alienation in turn can cause my co-researchers to feel insufficiently connected, and this condition—i.e., the lack of belongingness—is one of the important yet often overlooked causes of a variety of personal and social dysfunctions.

Belonging-ness is composed of active as well as passive elements, involving what you give as well as what you get. When you're very little, it's mainly a matter of feeling included by your family, it's passive. But when you get older, you become more aware that you can give, you can help, and you can be useful to those around you. When you make that kind of connection, you feel they belong to you as much as you belong to them. It's important for family to promote and validate this active component of belonging because it gives the feeling a deeper kind of rooted-ness.

The need to participate actively becomes even more important for my co-researchers. Organizations and communities can be inclusive; they can think they've helped people to feel they belong, but unless those folks can find some way to participate and give of themselves, they don't buy into the feeling. To say again, objective belonging (as observed from the outside) may not result in people feeling belongingness (deep inside).

Since the dynamic of belongingness hasn't been widely appreciated, some of its component elements haven't been widely understood. Nevertheless, a few people have addressed the interpersonal sphere in some practical ways.

Our culture does not talk about these dynamics partly because few understand it clearly, most people don't learn to realize what's going on inside them. Sure, words like loneliness, alienation, isolation, existential "angst," and other terms have been thrown around, but most people feel ashamed and guilty about being inadequate or otherwise personally deficient for feeling this way. Or they may feel resentment and yet don't know whom to blame. This may also be since much of our psychology has been oriented to the individual, implying that society is not to be challenged. The assumption still operates that healthy people can adjust and therefore that's what we should try to do.

The point to note, though, is that the hunger for belongingness, for human interchange, for feeling appreciated and the need for stroke exchange was for the most part overlooked not only by professionals, but was also not appreciated by clients and other people; the symptoms were not uncommon, but a good diagnosis in the sense of assessing the state of basic belongingness was rare.

Belonging-ness doesn't depend on any single source. In the world of the mind, there are several phenomena that are similarly the product of the overall sum of many inputs. Examples include the sense of self, the sense of meaning, the sense of spiritual connectedness, the sense of belonging-ness, among others.

If only my co-researchers feel more belongingness, they will tend to feel that their lives and experiences are more meaningful. Disconnection from belonging works in the opposite direction—they feel their lives become less meaningful, or even meaningless. This may also overlap with their sense of self. Some of my co-researchers lose self-esteem, feel ashamed, guilty, and reproach themselves, because they can't understand why they're so lonely or isolated. They tend to feel as if they could just will themselves into positive connectivity.

These children can learn a variety of ways to increase their capacity to make contacts and belong more. Learning these techniques, skills, and practices should be encouraged. However, equally important is the need for society and its sub-groups, businesses, communities, schools, and the like to take responsibility for welcoming and fostering connections among newcomers and those who don't easily fit in.

Spirituality is an interesting category: I define spirituality as the activity of developing one's connectedness or relationship with the greater wholeness of being, whether it is imagined as a personal supreme being, named or not, or as a less personal spirit or super-force of nature. The myths, stories, personages, scriptures, traditions, music, art, foods, and people all serve as psychological anchors, symbols that enhance the feeling of connection. Also, spirituality generally draws to it a sense of ultimate significance, deep meaning. So finding belongingness in one's relationship to the Divine Source also can be an important way to strengthen the process.

I define religion as the social organization of the spiritual impulse, and if people can further find a sense of belongingness with people who share their own connection or path, the whole complex further deepens and strengthens this dynamic in the psyche.

If there are insufficient emotional connections with other people, the mind will turn to secondary systems drawing on fantasy and illusion to maintain a sense of being in relationship, of belonging. My co-researchers can fill their lives with stuff but still be emotionally starved, and we hear their stories who crash and burn because of a lack of authentic psychological involvements. Unless we recognize the nature of the need to feel belongingness, they will not know how best to diagnose and correct the problem of belongingness-deficit.

This deficit can be marginal, so people can seem healthy enough to keep going. They live, though, without much vigor, they have little energy to give much more than what it takes just to stay alive, and there's little resilience to stress. People teetering on the edge of belongingness deficit feel un-ease, stress, but have not yet progressed to the point of fulfilling the criteria for a full dis-ease. Nor are they conscious of what's eating them.

One kind is the illusion of connectedness associated with possessions. Buying, stealing, manipulating, achieving, getting and then "having," collecting, accumulating—it can be not only things, but even celebrity, power or status. It seems as if these will gratify and satisfy, and they do, too, but only for a short burst. There's a little high, a kind of pseudo-belongingness, but then it fades. Drugs have this effect, too, and getting drunk and partying. Then you feel empty again and need another fix. As the sage in the Biblical book of Ecclesiastes says, "All is vanity."

Home is the single most important place for the children to feel accepted. The parents must embrace all their children with love and acceptance for being exactly who they are. Home is the first place for the children to learn about being accepted and accepting others. It is the parents' responsibility and privilege to create a nurturing environment where each child feels valued, safe, loved and whole.

Prostituted Male Street Children seeks a Nurturing Environment

In every society, babies are born helpless and ignorant and need older people to take care of them. In every society, babies must learn the local language and customs and form working relationships with the other members of their household. They must learn that the world has rules and that they cannot do whatever they feel like doing. This learning has to begin very early, at a time when they are still completely dependent on their adult caregivers.

There is no question that the adult caregivers play an important role in the baby's life. It is from these older people that babies learn their first language, have their first experiences in forming and maintaining relationships, and get their first lessons in following rules. But there are other conclusions: that what children learn in the early years about relationships and rules sets the pattern for later relationships and later rule-following, and hence determines the entire course of their lives.

I used to think so too. I still believe that children need to learn about relationships and rules in their early years; it is also important that they acquire a language. But I no longer believe that this early learning, which in our society generally takes place within the home, sets the pattern for what is to follow. Although the learning itself serves a purpose, the content of what children learn may be irrelevant to the world outside their home that they may cast it off when they step outside.

Today with increasing awareness among governmental and international agencies, the street children are seen especially as vulnerable group worthy of special interest, attention and intervention. But, despite existing programs and services for these vulnerable children, there is a continuous growth of victims who are prostituted silently like my co-researchers.

There are different sets of factors that may prompt a child to leave home. These factors could be grouped into categories like: economic factors such as poverty; a low standard of living; the child being sent to work at an early age; familial factors such as conflicts in the family, having a step-parent who is abusive, lack of love and attention; social factors such as pressure from peers to move away from home, attraction of city life as compared to the life of the rural areas; psychological factors such as the need to assert one's independence, the need for more attention, and so on.

The phenomenon of prostituted male street children is a repercussion of industrialization and urbanization. In the race for technological advancement, industrial growth centers have come up all over the world thus upsetting the age old patterns in which people lived and worked in their native villages and towns. The most crucial among such development induced patterns is the migration of people from rural to urban areas. Dwindling opportunities in the rural areas and the concomitant lure of life in towns and cities have resulted in a 'pull' towards the urban areas.

Their parents start migrating from relatively undeveloped regions of the country to the developing regions often leaving behind their families and homes. Their housing however, finds no place in the city's development plans. Uprooted from the only place they knew and could call their home, these people with a great deal of difficulty and rarely any social support, these migrant families barely manage a roof over their heads in slum clusters.

But, there is little that they can do for their children who wander on the streets while they work until late hours to make ends meet. Some children are fortunate to have a 'home' that they can retire to at the end of the day; many others have no other choice but to seek shelter on the pavements, in public places and so on.

It is not that children have to be on the streets because there is no space for them in the shanty that the parents might have managed to erect in the city. Often, the earnings of the parents are insufficient to secure even the family's most basic needs. Consequently, the children have to be sent to work to supplement the family's income.

Since these children are young, uneducated and unskilled they do not find work easily in the organized sector. Hence, they work largely in the unorganized sector and frequently end up in trades such as prostitution

It is not only economic compulsions that drive the children onto the streets. Social stratification based on caste, creed, gender, community, ethnicity, etc. also results in geographic, social, cultural and political compulsions. The economic compulsions are however, more directly visible and apparent than others.

All my co-researchers are school dropouts. They are forced to drop-out from school to work with their parents or to look after their younger siblings while their parents are at work. Most of the parents of my co-researchers don't support their educational needs because accordingly their parents survive life even they are elementary undergraduates. As a result, they may escape to the cities in the hope that they may be able to procure an education for themselves.

Most parents of my co-researchers still use the traditionally upheld methods of disciplining them by hitting them with belts, canes, sticks and so on. The young, gentle mind of a child is not designed to cope with such severe trauma and pain and when the situation becomes unbearable, the only escape the child knows is physical escape from the home - the source of the pain and torture.

The parents of my co-researchers get little opportunity to devote their time to their children. With both parents at work, the children go unattended for hours. In many cases, older siblings must look after the younger ones. There is too little for them to share by way of food and the younger ones do not always get their proper share. The neglected and deprived among the children feel not only insecure, but also unjustly treated. They may even doubt their parents' love for them. Thus, in a state of rejection and hurt, they may turn hostile and run away from home in search of other places where they belong and feel loved.

Since my co-researchers came from broken families, they are prone to emotional trauma and often suffer from feelings of rejection and insecurity that may drive them out in search of a place where they may be better accepted and loved.

Some of my co-researchers leave their homes for street life because of the influence of their peers. They find themselves on the streets because of their peers encouraging them to leave the conflict-ridden homes they live in. This is done by the peers glorifying the idea of city life, and independent life out of the home.

The media today also plays quite a significant role in the problem of children leaving home. Films typically dramatize, in an exaggerated fashion, the hero who leaves his home in the village, moves to the city and makes a fabulous life for himself. The newspapers, soap operas and other audio visual media over emphasize 'city life' as being 'exciting', 'adventurous', and 'totally filled with fun' and at the same time fail to realistically present the disadvantages of the same. Thus, children do not think twice about leaving their homes for the cities because they feel they will definitely have no problems with city life. Their illusions are shattered when they come into the cities, and they are then faced with the decision of admitting their mistake, giving up their pride and returning home or staying on in the city to prove themselves right.

My co-researchers live in an environment devoid of the affection, love, care and comfort of a family life. They are impelled by circumstances to struggle to fulfill their most basic needs like food and shelter at a very tender, impressionable age. They are deprived of all the things they covet in their childhood and are therefore aware of the chasm of difference that exists between them and 'normal' children.

Early on in life, they learn to make their own decisions in all matters since there is no one to help them or guide them. Most of all, they are physically & emotionally worn down by the need to fend for themselves and make a living at such a young age.

Even though my co-researchers can usually get some amount of food to eat, they do not have nutritious or balanced diets. This deficiency thus manifests itself in the form of anemia, malnutrition, and vitamin deficiencies. They who choose the streets as their home and face the most acute problems related to shelter. They are vulnerable to all ranges of weather conditions be it the burning heat of summer, the rainstorms and the cold nights. They do not suffer merely from physical homelessness, but also from a psychological homelessness since they have 'nowhere to belong.' The homes they leave behind no longer remain their havens; the streets provide no comfort, and society does not accept them.

My co-researchers live in an atmosphere of continued physical and mental strain. Many of them rummage through the garbage to find food; others go hungry for days drinking water or taking to drugs to diminish their pangs of hunger. All of them suffer from severe malnutrition and various kinds of deficiencies. The consumption of tobacco, alcohol and drugs retards their growth at an early age. Due to exposure to dust and other pollutants while they work near traffic junctions and other congested places, they suffer from bronchitis, asthma and even severe tuberculosis. Since they do not have the opportunity to bathe for several days at a time, and because of the unhygienic conditions in which they live, they are prone to skin diseases such as scabies, ulcers and rashes. They have limited knowledge about hygiene or Sexually Transmitted Diseases (STDs). Thus, they encounter sexual and reproductive health problems such as STDs.

The situations and events that lead my co-researchers to take to the streets may have an on-going impact on their well-being and may deprive them of emotional, economic, and other kinds of support for many successive years. The past also plays a role in predisposing them to become more vulnerable to emotional, social, and psychological disorders in the future. They frequently move from district to district, town to town, and city to city. In majority of instances, they do this by choice, but at other times, they are forced to keep moving to hide from the police, welfare authorities, and gangsters. This evasive lifestyle results in problems of social isolation and loneliness and leads to difficulties in developing emotional attachments to other human beings.

All my co-researchers resort to using psychoactive substances (such as alcohol and drugs) to escape from the overwhelming pressure of their traumatic past and their daily problems. This, in turn, can lead to medical problems due to overdoses, an increase in the probability of accidents, violence and unprotected sex. Over time, it can lead to complications such as brain and liver damage, as also to diseases like HIV / AIDS.

My co-researchers learn a set of moral values and moral behaviour in their early years of family life. They begin to live on the streets soon realize that the values their family taught them (such as honest, integrity, etc.) are not conducive to their survival on the streets. At times they are forced to steal food and money because they have none of their own. They have to swallow their pride in order to beg for food or money. They learn to live without a daily bath, in unhygienic and unsanitary conditions. They learn to let go of their shame when they have no clothes.

The varied needs of my co-researchers are rarely met. They frequently go hungry, wear torn, tattered and dirty clothes. They have no permanent place to stay, no educational facilities, no facilities for hygiene and in brief, no facilities at all. Psychologically, they are exploited and abused, thus their basic needs of security and happiness are not met. Socio-culturally, they lack opportunities for healthy recreation and lack social acceptance. They must work to survive. Since they have no skills with which to bargain for fair pay or to fight for their rights, they are very vulnerable to employers who look to make a profit on them. Frequently, they are forced to work for 10-12 hours a day for very meager payment or in exchange for just one square meal a day. Besides all this, abuse and harassment - either physical or sexual, by persons in authority, be they police personnel or others is not uncommon.

Besides the police, the street children are frequently taken advantage of by the underworld gangsters or by older street boys who bully them and use them to achieve their own ends. If they do not oblige, they are threatened and beaten.

People in society generally perceive my co-researchers as difficult children who are out to cause trouble. The general misconception is that they are addicts, uncontrollable and violent, have no emotions or moral values, and so on. Because of these misconceptions, people tend to be unsympathetic and indifferent to the actual plight of children on the street. This lack of social acceptance is what pushes them away from mainstream society and forces them to survive on the fringes of the social system.

Eidetic Insight

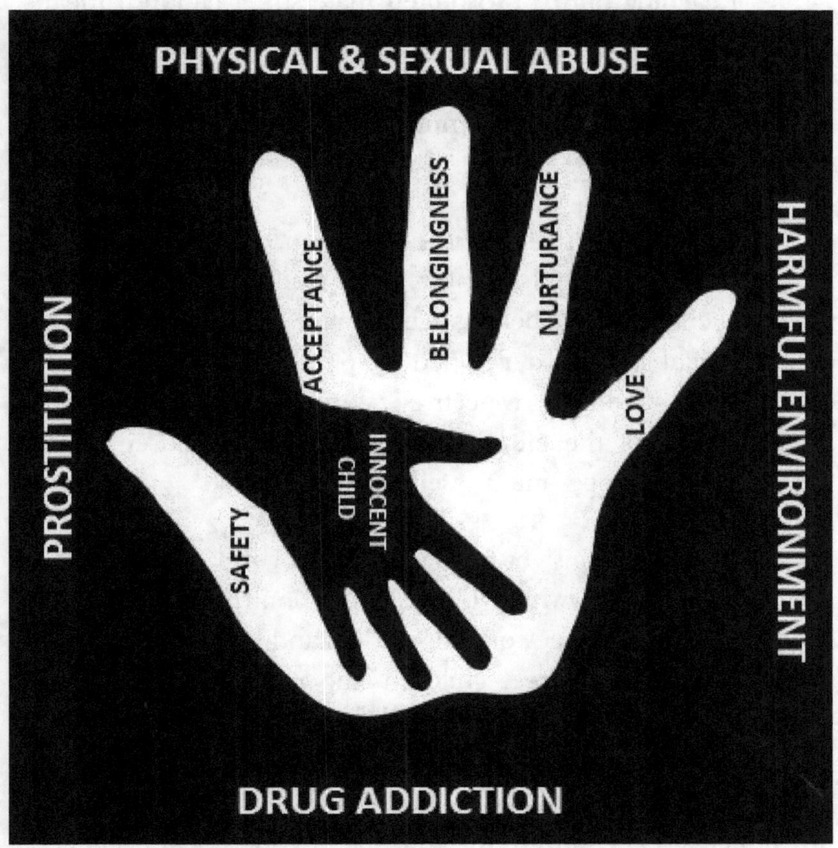

Figure 70. Symbol of my Eidetic Insight: Reaching out to prostituted male street children

Expounding my eidetic insight:

Reaching out to prostituted male street children means providing them opportunities for growth and development and showing them that they are loved, accepted, secured, nurtured and are assured of belongingness.

Prostituted male street children, no matter how miserable they feel, still long for such significant needs as love, acceptance, security, belongingness and nurturance. This eidetic insight which I developed after reflecting on the various themes from their respective stories is my conscious understanding of the life of these male street children. This made me look deeper into myself.

My eidetic insight is the essence of the social facts. It reflects a key point which I consider a contribution from my study. It is like a framework for understanding the experiences of male prostituted street children, the pure essence of their reality. The framework is symbolized by the figure shown which I entitled, "reaching out to prostituted male street children." I relate this to my understanding of the reality or situation of male prostituted street children who must be provided better services.

Prostituted children seek support from someone who can lend a hand or who can give them a chance to have a better future. Despite existing government and non-government programs and services intended for them, it seems that their number is increasing fast silently. There are agencies that give them opportunity for growth, but without acceptance, belongingness, security, love, and nurturance, we just let them hold our hands and let them look for someone who can provide them their longing for their needs in ways that may harm them further.

CHAPTER 4

CREATIVE SYNTHESIS

Early on in life, my co-researchers learned to make their own decisions in all matters since there is no one to help and guide them. Most of all, they are physically and emotionally-worn down by the need to fend for themselves and make a living at such a young age. They have difficult time in life for self-consciousness and discomfort with oneself. At their very young age, they develop anxiety; they encounter new stresses that lack adequate coping skills to deal with.

The innocence of my co-researchers were shattered, causing a deep feeling of shame, poisoning the sense of self and excluding them from education, friends and the broader society. They don't yet have well-developed boundaries and a sense of self. For these reasons, they become vulnerable target for a sexual predator and other sexually-confused adult who has not developed their own appropriate boundaries and sense of morality. Their experiences may have resulted in their viewing trust as something to be earned, not given, so therefore they withhold trust from others until they are sure they deserve it. Having a low propensity to trust can hold them back from experiencing true joy and fulfillment in relationships.

Despite these experiences, my co-researchers acknowledged and recognized their own internal and external strengths. They believed that not all pain is bad in the moral sense. God created us with nerve endings that use pain to protect us.

All my co-researchers came from broken families that earn less and experience lower levels of educational achievement. Worse, they pass the prospect of meager incomes and family instability on to their children, ensuring a continuing if not expanding cycle of economic distress. By its very nature, broken family, changes not only the structure of the family but also its dynamics. Most of them experience loss of their father which have long-term effects on their life and cannot be compensated by the mother or other relative. The parents of my co-researchers get little opportunity to devote their time to their children. They are neglected and deprived which made them feel not only insecure, but also unjustly treated. They even doubt their parents' love for them. Thus, in a state of rejection and hurt, they turn hostile and run away from home in search of other places where they may belong and feel loved.

The main role of their parents should be to provide care and prepare their child for independent survival as an adult. They must embrace all their children with love and acceptance for being exactly who they are. Home is the first place for the children to learn about being accepted and accepting others. It is the parent's responsibility and privilege to create a nurturing environment where each child feels valued, safe, loved and whole. God organizes us into families so that we can grow up in happiness and safety, and so that we can learn to love others selflessly but sadly, my co-researchers experienced deficits in emotional development. They seem tearful and depressed from their different experiences in terms of their family issues.

Low standard of living has more tendencies for them to engage in prostitution; that's why it's important that parents should give them proper upbringing and necessary financial provisions so that they will not look for alternative ways to make up for their shortfalls; and, hence, predisposed to prostitution tendencies. Adults are seen by children as social pillars and should be taught right values, morals, attitudes, and behavior of life.

People in society generally perceive my co-researchers as difficult children who are out to cause trouble. The general misconception is that they are addicts, uncontrollable and violent, have no emotions or moral values, and so on. Because of these misconceptions, people tend to be unsympathetic and indifferent to the actual plight of children on the street. This lack of social acceptance is what pushes them away from mainstream society and forces them to survive on the fringes of the social system.

My co-researchers suffer from painful feeling of isolation. In their search for a sense of group belonging, they become vulnerable to the influence of delinquent and child prostitution. They are frequently taken advantage of by the underworld gangsters and by older street boys who bully them and use them to achieve their own ends. If they do not oblige, they are threatened and beaten. They are influenced by their peers and motivated to live in the street and entertain gay strangers to earn a living in the community.

Accordingly, peer influence isn't all bad. It shows that among peers they can find friendship and acceptance and able to share their experiences that can build lasting bonds. Peers can help them in decision-making; they can give opportunities to try out new social skills, and can encourage them to fight to live. But because of this, they developed little faith in their own abilities to achieve interpersonal goals.

There are many reasons for a child to engage in prostitution. Some of my co-researchers have stated that they are attracted by the large sums of money they can earn while they are still young. They also see themselves as a helping hand to their mothers to provide the basic need of the family. They view prostitution as their way out of poverty. While they may choose to sell themselves, it is economic necessity that drives them. Most of them cannot depend on parental or familial assistance as their options are limited. They are forced to pursue child prostitution and use their internal strengths to navigate this often precarious and hazardous street environment.

They tried to look for other means to end prostitution but unable to get jobs and are sometimes pressured because they are the only bread winners in the family. Most of them intended to leave prostitution and tried to beg/plead in the street to earn a living but despite this means, it's still insufficient for them to provide their needs and wants. In fact, all of my co-researchers wanted out, but lack viable alternatives. They are unable to leave because of their addiction or the need to feed their family.

Unfortunately, exploiters know vulnerable children have few choices; hence, they manipulate them by promising that they will fill the voids of missing love, protection, and basic needs like food, clothing, and shelter. Humiliation, shame and fear equal silence. These emotions cause that response to my co-researchers. Offenders reinforce these feelings by the things they say and do to the prostituted child. Sometimes, they may be confused if they experience positive physical pleasure, arousal, or emotional intimacy from engaging sexual contact. This confusion can make it difficult for them to speak up.

All my co-researchers resort to using psychoactive substances such as alcohol and drugs to escape from the overwhelming pressure of their traumatic past and their daily problems.

An innocent child is propelled by their skills and knowledge, with this limited capacity, they have difficulty in propelling their lives. They have no choice but to survive living in the street that can lead them to harmful and dangerous experiences such as prostitution. Their peers can damage their lives by negative influence in adapting to their environment. Since they are innocent, peers had advantages that can lure them from different vices and engaging prostitution to sustain these addictions.

The social work profession is committed to the values of human dignity, personal autonomy, self-realization and self-determination. These are the very areas that are most severely damaged in the lives of the victims. As a social worker, we must integrate different core values to be able to provide effective and holistic approaches in helping the prostituted children.

Social Worker must respect the inherent dignity, worth, beauty and creativity of each child. Respect is important in the context of social work. We should take efforts to understand the child to create a respectful, professional relationship. Establishing a respectful relationship with a street child is therefore imperative in not only increasing their self-worth but encouraging them to engage with services and society. Social Worker must believe that meaningful and nurturing relationships facilitate transformation and personal growth of a child. A child's early experience of being nurtured develops a bond with a caring society that affects all aspects of behavior and development.

Children need to experience a safe, welcoming and encouraging environment for their participation. The quality of children's participation and their ability to benefit from it are strongly influenced by the efforts made to create a positive environment.

The creative synthesis of my study is described and demonstrated by the image below:

Figure 71. Symbolic Representation of my creative synthesis

Figure 72. The boat symbolizes an innocent child

I expound below the meaning of each aspect in my creative synthesis:

The boat is a small vessel propelled on water by oars, sails or an engine. It symbolizes an innocent child who is propelled by their skills and knowledge. However, given their limited capacity, they have difficulty in propelling their lives. They have no choice but to go with the flow of waters that can lead them to harmful and dangerous experiences such as prostitution. Prostituted children are typically found in depressed communities like a small boat found on inland lakes. Because of limited opportunities that can transform their lives, they tend to get lost and live in misery. Boats have a wide variety of shapes, sizes and construction methods due to their intended purpose like an innocent child. They have a wide variety of experiences that molds them to engage in prostitution. They have different experiences and lives with different purposes. Some of them earn a living for the sake of their family. They want to support their parents and siblings. Some of them are hopelessly surviving while some are trying to voice out the realistic phenomenon of being a prostituted child.

Figure 73. The water symbolizes life in the street

Water: The water is a colorless, transparent, odorless, tasteless liquid that form in the lake. It symbolizes the street life in the community. Living in the street to be able to survive is as plain as the water. You go with the flow of life where your path and destiny is headed. The community has a huge impact to the lives of an innocent child. It has a big influence on them which can destroy their lives or can make them functional individuals in the society.

Crow: The crow is a bird that may frequently cause damage to crops and property, strew trash, and transfer disease. In my study, it symbolizes the peers who influenced an innocent child. Crows are like other street children that gather near large food sources such as garbage dumps and shopping centers. They are smart and can well adjust in their environment which makes them adaptable

Figure 74. The crow symbolizes peers

and opportunistic. Crows, like the peers who are likewise street children, can damage an innocent child by negative influence in adapting to their environment. Since the child is innocent, peers have the advantage to lure them from different vices and engage in prostitution to sustain these addictions.

Tree: A tree is a woody perennial plant, typically having a single stem or trunk growing to a considerable height and bearing lateral branches at some distance from the ground. The tree symbolizes the perpetrators who victimized an innocent child. Trees are tall and their woods give structural strength to their body like the adult perpetrators who are big, powerful, more intelligent that can victimize an innocent child.

Figure 75. The tree symbolizes the perpetrators who victimized innocent children

Diamonds are precious stones consisting of a clear and typically colorless crystalline form of pure carbon, the hardest naturally occurring substance. It symbolizes money and temptations. An innocent child can grab this diamond in exchange of anything to be able to survive and sustain their vices as influenced by their peers. Since it is scattered in the illustration, it means that money and temptation is around the community including the people that

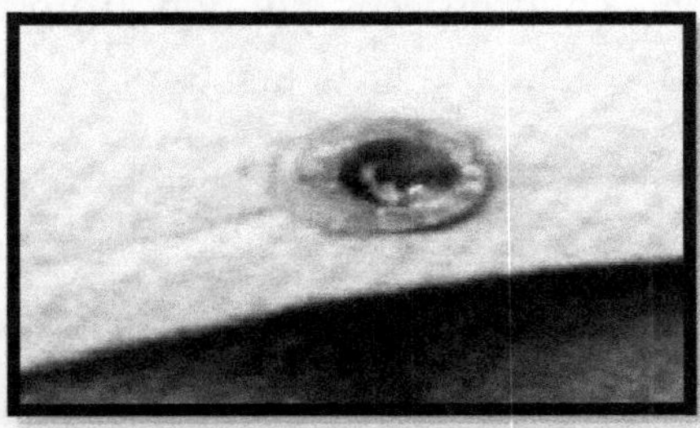

Figure 76. The diamond symbolizes money and temptation

can nurture them. These are money that can be earned in the streets through scavenging, begging, and prostitution or a temptation to steal things from others. In this sense, an innocent child can be easily attracted to these temptations such that some can ruin their lives.

Figure 77. Dock symbolizes reaching out to the innocent children

Dock is a structure extending alongshore into a body of water, to which boats may be moored. It symbolizes the "opportunity to reach out" to the innocent children who need someone to moor them and who they can lean on and get support. In this sense, prostituted children seek support from someone who can lend a hand and give them a chance to have a better future.

Figure 78. The flowers symbolize acceptance, love, nurturance and safe place

Flower is the seed-bearing structure or part found in plants consisting of reproductive organs (stamens and carpels) which symbolizes both parents. It denotes acceptance, love, nurturance and most importantly, a safe place for a prostituted child to be. Parents are significant in a child's growth. The absence of one parent can affect a child's situation entirely. Despite the existing government and non-government programs and services, the number of prostituted children seems to be rapidly increasing. Yes, as a change agent, we may be able to give them opportunity for growth; but, without these flowers (parents), we just let them lean on the dock and most probably get back to the shore to seek someone who can provide them acceptance, love, nurture and protection in a different way.

CHAPTER 5

IMPLICATIONS TO SOCIAL WORK PROFESSION

The social work profession is committed to the values of human dignity, personal autonomy, self-realization and self-determination. These are the very areas that are severely damaged in the life of the victims in this study.

In the social work profession, it is imperative that the following core values are integrated to provide effective and holistic approaches in helping prostituted children.

Respect for Dignity: "We must respect the inherent dignity, worth, beauty and creativity of each child."

Respect is important in the context of social work. Respect should not be confused with obedience or tolerance but rather efforts should be placed on learning to understand the child to create a respectful, professional relationship.

Many street children we work with receive very little respect in their social encounters due to the clothes they wear, the way they talk, or their inability to read and write. I am a witness to the way they are treated, discriminated and belittled daily by shop assistants, bank clerks and other professionals who should know better. Respectful behaviour cannot come easily to people who are almost never shown it themselves.

Establishing a respectful relationship with a street child is therefore imperative not only to increase their self-worth but to encourage them to engage in societal services. It is the starting point for social inclusion. Using discretion and theory and communicating with that individual enables to ascertain mutual respectful boundaries.

Through practice and observation of those who I respect, there are some basics to establish a respectful relationship. Listening to the child is very important. In doing so, one must be as honest and open as possible so they know what actions are taking and why. Acknowledge the power difference between you and be clear from the start what your role is and what your role is not.

Gaining respect should remain a fresh challenge with every new child we meet and it begins with us, as social workers, being respectful to them.

Nurturing Relationship: "We must believe that meaningful and nurturing relationships facilitate transformation and personal growth of a child."

A child's early experience of being nurtured develops a bond with a caring social worker. This nurturance affects all aspects of behavior and development. If the social worker and the child have strong, warm feelings for one another, the child will develop trust towards their social workers who provides what they need to thrive, including love, acceptance, positive guidance, and protection.

Building a nurturing, close relationship involves a lot of tender, loving care. The basics include being loving and affectionate with the child, understanding and responding to their needs, doing things together, talking, being involved and interested in their activities, and being aware of their friendships and interests.

We should also have programs and initiatives that support parents as they work to develop close, nurturing relationships with their children.

Most importantly, recognize that opportunities to connect with a child are ever-present. Sometimes a sports outdoor activity, summer camps, outings, or a mountain climbing can spark conversations that help social worker and the child stay in tune with each other.

Improving clients' relationships with social worker has important, positive and long-lasting implications for both client and social development. Solely improving clients' relationships with their social workers will not produce gains in achievement. However, these children who have close, positive and supportive relationships with their social workers will attain higher levels of transformation than those children with more conflict in their relationships.

Picture a child who feels a strong personal connection with his social worker, talks with his social worker frequently, and receives more constructive guidance and praise rather than just criticism. The children is likely to trust his social worker more, show more engagement in learning, and behave better in the center and motivated to pursue his dreams. Positive client-worker relationships draw children into the process of transformation and promote their desire to transform.

Participation and Empowerment: "We must promote the participation of children in all decisions concerning them, and we must empower children and parents to take responsibility for their own lives"

Participation is about having the opportunity to express a view, influencing decision-making and achieving change. Children's participation is an informed and willing involvement of all children, including the most marginalized and those of different ages and abilities, in any matter concerning them either directly or indirectly. Children's participation is a way of working and an essential principle that cuts across all programs and takes place in all arenas – from home to government, from local to international levels.

Social workers are committed to ethical participatory practice and to the primacy of children's best interests. There are inevitable imbalances in power and status between social workers and children. An ethical approach is needed for children's participation to be genuine and meaningful.

Street children can freely express their views and opinions and have them treated with respect. There is clarity of purpose about children's participation and honesty about its parameters. Children understand how much impact they can have on decision-making and who will make the final decision.

The roles and responsibilities of all involved (children and social worker) are clearly outlined, understood and agreed upon.

Clear goals and targets are agreed upon with the children concerned. Children are provided with, and have access to, relevant information regarding their involvement. Children are involved from the earliest possible stage and can influence the design and content of participatory processes. Social workers involved in any participatory processes are sensitized to working with children, clear about their role and willing to listen and learn. Organizations and social workers are accountable to children for the commitments they make. Where the process of involvement requires representation from a wider group of children, the selection of representatives will be based on principles of democracy and non-discrimination. The barriers and challenges that participating children may have faced in other spheres of their lives are considered and discussed with the children involved to reduce any potential negative impacts from their participation.

The information and insights that children must have about their own lives and their communities are issues that affect them. Recognizing their other commitments, children participation must be on their own terms and for lengths of time chosen by them. The issues must be of real relevance to the children who are being involved and draw upon their knowledge, skills and abilities. Children are usually involved in setting the criteria for selection and representation for participation.

Support from key adults in children's lives (eg, parents/guardians, teachers) is gained to ensure wider encouragement and assistance for the participation of the child.

To develop a culture of participation there must first be open discussion between managers, social workers and children and young people in which they define participation and recognize its importance. Establishing a definition should involve agreement on aims, objectives and outcomes along with a shared understanding of the extent to which children will be involved in decisions.

Before social workers, children and young people can make a considered decision about the need for participation, they need to understand why participation should be integral to the workings of the organisation. They can do this by gaining understanding of the legislative requirements of participation.

It is important that children, young people and social workers all have a good understanding of the decision-making processes in place so they can establish where power lies and the points where it needs to change.

This is a sensitive process which must take on board the expectations and anxieties of social workers as well as establishing a consensus on where the boundaries of young people's involvement should be. This includes evaluating which decisions and actions can be exposed to change and how and to what extent young people can be involved in the process or parts of it.

Child-Friendly Environment: "We must create a child-friendly environment where children are safe and have space to play"

Children need to experience a safe, welcoming and encouraging environment for their participation. The quality of children's participation and their ability to benefit from it are strongly influenced by the efforts made to create a positive environment for their participation.

Creating a safe environment for children is a dynamic process that involves active participation and responsibility by all sectors of the community – individuals, families, government and non-government organizations and community groups. Sharing responsibility for the care and protection of children helps to develop a stronger, more child-focused community. A child-safe community can: care for all children; identify vulnerable children; support children who have been abused and neglected; and prevent further harm to children. The focus of a child-safe organization is not simply to create an environment that minimizes risk or danger. Rather it is about building an environment which is both child-safe and child-friendly, where children feel respected, valued and encouraged to reach their full potential.

A child safe environment is the product of a range of strategies and initiatives. In addition to child-safe policies and appropriate codes of conduct and behavior for social workers, volunteers and members, organizations must foster cultures of openness. This means children need to know what to do if they believe they have been subject to inappropriate behavior or have experienced abuse. The organizations need to have very clear procedures to assist social workers/volunteers in identifying suspected abuse and neglect. The management, social workers and volunteers must also be aware of their duty to report suspected abuse and neglect to the families and take other measures to establish, promote and maintain child-safe and child-friendly environments.

Social worker must be knowledgeable of different ways in building the self-esteem and self-confidence of the child of different ages and abilities so they will feel they can contribute and that they have valid experience and views to contribute. Methods of involvement of social worker are developed in partnership with children so that they reflect their preferred mediums of expression. Social workers assure sufficient time and resources are made available for quality participation and children are properly supported to prepare for their participation. Social workers are sensitized to understand the value of children's participation and are enabled to play a positive role in supporting it.

Child-friendly meeting places are used where children feel relaxed, comfortable and have access to the facilities they need. The meeting places must be accessible to children with disabilities. Organizational or official procedures are designed/modified to facilitate (rather than intimidate) children and make less experienced children feel welcome.

We need to provide support where necessary to share information and/or build skills and capacity to enable children, individually and collectively, to participate effectively

"A Male Prostituted Child, Callboy"
(A musical composition)

This is a sad story that is full of pain,
Like a question that can't be answered in a crumpled paper.
I feel bad for myself and eaten by fear.
I have been drowned for a long time
that turned my world upside down
Just to provide simple needs
in exchange of my body for sex.
I tried to avoid it but I have no choice.
I overused my body which was labeled by others
A temptation that destroyed a lot of lives
and ruined their dreams.
Life challenges are really difficult
But you need to stand even when you fall.

I can't paint my future because of the risk I take.
I will remove shame within me just to cut the curse.
The curse that is feared by most people
You will lose trust for yourself
Because of the only sin that you committed
that cannot be corrected even if you regret it.
Why can't people escape difficulties in life?
Is it because they don't think about it?

You tried everything to lead a normal life
You don't even like it but you are fallen to a trap
that can cause death.
What is going to happen if this does not end?
In that question, I will leave it to God.

This is the last chapter of my revelation.
I will reveal everything to make it fair.
I prepare my own body and life
So that I can dance with the waves of life
I am a male child that they used to call a callboy
For the same gender, my body was ruined
since I was an innocent child
Even myself I tried to abandon
Just to forget everything what happened
Where in a situation that I fall asleep
with empty stomach
I didn't mean to do it in this way
All I want is not to be judged.

I am not expecting all these to happen
That this will be a sin
I didn't mean to do those things
I'm just a child who is a victim.

www.ingramcontent.com/pod-product-compliance
Lightning Source LLC
LaVergne TN
LVHW050627200726
843506LV00010B/1154